Dedication

'FOR CORDELL'

BLOTTO

ADVENTURES & MISADVENTURES IN PSYCHEDELIA

Table of Contents

Foreword 1
Acknowledgements: 4
INITIATION 11
GETTING HIGHER EDUCATION 20
UMBILICAL DISCORD 32
MIDNIGHT SEXPRESS 37
ON THE ROAD AGAIN 42
NO-FAULT OF SAN ANDREAS 51
MUM'S THE WORD 55
KRITI CALL 62
STRAWBERRY FIELDS 71
FREE WAY 76
TROUBLE IN PARADISE 91
THE BAGMAN'S OM 101
UNIDENTIFIED FLYING OBJET D' ART 108
BACK TO BLIGHTY 117
IN - HOUSE DIVERSIONS 121
GO WEST 128
RUNNIN' REBELS 136
IGNITION 139
GEISERVILLE 152
GATHERING STORM CLOUDS 159
GOLDEN JUBILEE 162

SNARED	172
BANGED UP	181
THE PLOT THICKENS	189
DENOUEMENT	198
VANITY BLOTTER	201
JOURNEYING IN THE FUTURE	205

Foreword

Books about LSD and the culture surrounding it tend to be written mainly by historians, biographers, journalists, scientists, and ex-police officers; outsiders looking in on a scene which fascinates but to which they have only a tangential connection. So when you first set eyes on a copy of Blotto, you would be forgiven for thinking, Kevin who? Who indeed, because until the publication of this book, British-born Kevin Barron was an enigma, his identity and activities are known only to a handful of people in the global psychedelic community, which is exactly how he wanted it, for reasons that will become clear as you read the book.

After a serendipitous encounter with LSD in his late teens, courtesy of a 200-mic dose of pure Sandoz acid, Kevin embarked on a kaleidoscopic psychedelic journey which took him deep into the heart of the psychedelic scene. A formal career in Fine Art, which he studied at a degree level, beckoned initially, but the fates had other plans for Kevin and a combination of happenstance, and his love of music found him steering the 1968 Isle of Wight festival from being a potential financial disaster to a resounding success. His organisational skills and ability to wrangle very stoned musicians led to a friendship with Jefferson Airplane, further musical adventures in Britain with artists such as Cat Stevens, and a side hustle into London property development. So far, so weird, but then he lands the gig as the logistics manager on the Rolling Stones' 1973 tour of Australia and New Zealand. Kevin's account of his exploits in the world of rock music alone would be enough to form a book in themselves. But there is more, much more.

Kevin's love of fine art and psychedelics came together perfectly when he was asked to create a design for sheets of blotter destined to be soaked with LSD in Japan. Blotter acid was in its infancy at this time, and this was Kevin's first foray into the burgeoning world of creative LSD blotter designs. He excelled at it, and his passion for art and LSD opened new and lucrative opportunities as word of his talents spread, and he quickly became immersed in the intricate warp and weft of the international world of LSD blotter design, manufacture, and smuggling.

Demand for Kevin's blotter designs increased, and over the years, he created numerous classic blotters, including the legendary Knights Templar Shield, Strawberry Fields, 1993 Jubilee, and my personal favourite, the simple but iconic flying saucers. If you are a veteran LSD aficionado,, you will almost certainly have eaten several pieces of Kevin's artwork.

As his story unfolds Kevin meets with a variety of remarkable men, movers and shakers of the acid world, some of whose names will be familiar, such as Rick Griffin or Mark McCloud but also many others of no less importance but whose true identities have been obscured for obvious reasons; LSD manufacturing chemists and their ilk, men whose lysergic chemical alchemy has blown millions of minds and thus subtly affected the course of history.

Along the way, you'll meet Kevin in several other guises, including Kevin the epicure and restaurateur, and, just when you think his life can't get any stranger, he discovers MDMA and realises it's a drug perfectly tooled to mesh with the rapidly developing house music scene in Britain. In a stroke of genius, he introduces British house music DJs to the West Coast of America, ensuring the debut event was fuelled with a healthy supply of acid and molly.

Eventually, Kevin's world comes crashing down in London when he is caught in a police sting, becoming a prisoner of the war on drugs. But even then, as you will read, he makes the best of a tricky situation, playing the authorities at their own game. Now long since retired from his career as a designer of blotter destined to become 'live', Kevin is recognised as a world-renowned creator of blotter art, un-dosed perforated sheets with the most intricate and subtle designs and images. His work has been exhibited in several countries and his blotter art is sought after and eagerly collected by connoisseurs of this fascinating art form.

This Foreword is simply to put Kevin's remarkable life in context, to show how he has spanned, with psychedelic purpose, the decades from the sixties onwards and the impact he has had on the development of psychedelic culture. I hope I have whetted your appetite to read about Kevin's life, which, like the LSD experience itself, is labyrinthine and rich with anecdotes. If I had given the impression that Kevin is a name-dropping international jet setter, nothing could be further from the truth. After months of email communications, I first met Kevin at the 2023 Breaking Convention event in Exeter, England. I found him to be self-effacing, witty, warm, and compassionate, exactly the traits you'd expect to find in someone who has devoted his life and talents to spreading the message of LSD. Now read on…

Andy Roberts
Holywell
February 2024

Acknowledgements:

"This book is dedicated to the following individuals, 'The KEEPERS OF THE FLAME' who sacrificed their liberty in their fundamental belief that LSD and all psychedelics provide a gateway to a deeper reality and are positive tools for all humankind.

Owsley Stanley, Tim Scully, Nicholas Sand, Richard Kemp, Alston Hughes, William Leonard Pickard.

I am eternally grateful to Andy Roberts for his forward to the book.

Thank you to David Elalouf for his back cover photograph.

Email : davidelalouf@gmail.com

A personal thank you to Mark McCloud for introducing to the broader world LSD blotter art.

That first Monday in September 1993 marked the beginning of another Indian summer in London, one of those perfectly transparent 20/20 vision days exaggerating the already stark three-dimensionality of the garden square's uniform Georgian buildings. Two months earlier, on our return from Greece, Eleanor and I had taken a summer letting of the first-floor flat at number 13. It wasn't superstition but a more intuitive general unease that we felt that morning. Focused minds and a concerted effort were required to complete the task before sunrise, yet a sense of discomfort lingered. The client wasn't expected before five that evening: our Tuesday morning New York-bound flight seats had been confirmed…. What could go wrong?

Recharged with double espressos, we elected to distance ourselves from the scene of our nocturnal labour. Some last-minute shopping seemed the ideal distraction from any niggling concerns. We scurried from the flat, headed toward Fulham Road and came to a halt outside the pretentiously named stationer, "Papyrus." The storefront window showcased an array of signets and assorted coloured sealing wax. Has adhesive envelopes become obsolete?

"Let me see, I'll use the red wax for the overdue telephone bill and the silver for the 'Platinum' Visa card statement."

The interior shelves were decorated with embossed gold leaf wedding invitations, a crocodile skin ink blotter, and personal diaries for babies (ideal for a precocious two-year-old). We were looking for distinctive and appropriate wrapping paper that reflected a personal touch.

"Wow! Check it out, honey! It's totally awesome."

Eleanor's faux 'valley talk' drew a contemptuous glare from the Sloane Ranger shop assistant. For a feisty Southern Californian, Eleanor had the rare ability to recognize an English snob and dealt deftly with her.

"Would you mind terribly holding this up for me to view closer?" Eleanor enquired.

The layout of the wrapping paper, similar to the shellfish posters that seem de rigueur at respectable fishmongers, adorned the bicycle's pictorial history. It was perfect.

"We'll take it. Oh, and if you wouldn't mind, we'd like it gift-wrapped".

After an alfresco lunch at a Chelsea trattoria, we caught a cab back to Kensington, paid the driver off at the corner and strolled arm in arm towards number 13.

Maybe it was the effects of the wine over lunch as our earlier anxieties had receded. Our conversation had drifted towards restaurants in New York. We were just two doors from the house when I glanced skyward, squinting in the glare of the now-hazy sunshine. I opened my eyes, refocusing to see Eleanor and I encircled by a dozen plain-clothed police. One flashed a badge and muttered something, but my thoughts raced elsewhere.

Turning and looking up at the first-floor balcony, my mind zoomed beyond the French windows into the living room. Scanning the interior, I closed in on the patinated oak chest, on top of which lay a neatly stacked pile of A4 paper. Each sheet was emblazoned with a bicycle pattern resembling postage stamps and perforated into a thousand quarter-inch squares. Each tiny square had absorbed 100 micrograms of pure liquid Lysergic Acid Diethylamide… LSD.

The two-inch thick pile contained 50,000 doses of the drug. I switched my focus to the kitchen, and a sealed glass conical flask stood on the refrigerator's shelf. The contents, a colourless liquid, contained a solution of a further 100.000 doses. I thought about the cardboard cartons in the bedroom containing nearly three thousand sheets of 'bicycle 'Blotter paper. Enough to absorb almost three million more doses of LSD. I ignored the few comparatively inconsequential grams of marijuana lying on the living room coffee table.

One hears of individuals surviving near-death experiences and how they witness their life history as a nanosecond flashback. Mind rewound and came to an abrupt halt in 1964 outside the door to the office of the headmaster of Portsmouth Southern Grammar School.

Beginning with the reign of King Henry VIII, the wealth and economy of the city of Portsmouth had been intrinsically linked to the Royal Navy. The dockyard had continuously been the primary employer, and to accommodate the 'Senior Service', the city boasted more brothels and pubs per square mile than anywhere in the United Kingdom. Portsmouth's only other sizable source of revenue came in the summer months from tourists and day trippers, the pebbled beach affording them a panoramic view of the Isle of Wight and the Solent waterway. As a child, I witnessed the passage of the great ocean-going liners as they sailed out into the English Channel on their westbound transatlantic voyages to New York and other faraway exotic destinations. Some of my happiest childhood memories were of times during the summer months spent at the beach during school lunch breaks. I would bicycle to the esplanade, joining the family for a picnic and a quick dip in the sea.

To this day, I've never understood my mother's insistence that after eating, I should always wait twenty minutes before venturing into the sea. What terrible fate awaited me after only nineteen?

Saturday evenings were routine, spent at the local church youth club, which, for some inexplicable reason, always had an abundance of girls in attendance, none of whom appeared particularly devout. Moreover, any liaison with anyone god-fearing would invariably mean enduring the tedium of the church sermon the following morning.

Besides the usual indoor sporting activities, the club ran a weekly disco that, in reality, was a misnomer for an old 'Dansette' record player with a continuous feed of half a dozen seven-inch 45 rpm vinyl discs. This was the meeting point. The problem was that the girls only ever seemed to want to dance with one another whilst the frustrated males stood with their backs to the wall, attempting to impress the fairer sex by playing air guitar to the tinny sound of early Stax and Motown soul music. A sickly fermentation of Cyprus Cream Sherry smuggled onto the premises and consumed from teacups provided some 'Dutch courage'.

This was the only respite from the drudgery of Grammar school and academia, which seemed to occupy most of my waking hours. The weeknights were mainly spent hunched over volumes of school textbooks, vainly attempting to conjugate Latin verbs or comprehend the laws of physics. I would relax only after bed, tucking myself under the bedcovers with a portable radio tuned to 'Radio Luxembourg.' Unfortunately, and infuriatingly, the reception was always poor, and the signal constantly faded in and out. Still, in the early 1960s, this was the only station playing cutting-edge contemporary music.

I had been at the Grammar School for six years, yet this was to be my first face-to-face encounter with Henry Mills, the headmaster. I suppose I was just an anonymous pupil, neither academically outstanding to warrant his personal accolades nor undisciplined to justify welts from one of his infamous thrashings. His reputation as a practitioner in the finer art of corporal punishment was ignominious. His implement of choice was a mature, flexed bamboo cane with a frayed tip. The target zone was randomly selected— either the palm of the non-writing hand or the buttocks. Any boy caught padding his pants would receive a bonus of six lashes across the hand. Mills was an imposing Dickensian figure with Neanderthal facial features, dishevelled jet-black hair, bushy eyebrows, and curiously, tufts sprouted from his pronounced cheekbones. In all my years at the school, he wore the same crumpled tweed jacket beneath a threadbare black gown. My stomach churned as I tentatively wrapped my knuckle around the panelled mahogany door.

"Enter!" a voice bellowed from the inner sanctum.

Once granted access, there was a hard and fast rule: a pupil was to wait by the door until summoned forward to Mill's desk. This delay allowed one to indulge in the school ritual of scuffing with one's shoes on the border of the priceless Persian carpet that stretched the length of the study. Mills sat at his desk, scanning a file. The tweed jacket now bore distressed brown leather elbow patches.

"Step forward, boy! Well, Barron. Sandhurst! You won't regret the decision."

What the hell was he talking about? A career in the military had never been considered.

"Excuse me, sir. Sandhurst? The British Army's officer academy?"

"I've just been studying your school record, Barron. You've spent five years in the school's Combined Cadet Force. You're a ranked N.C.O. and the school's armourer. All the groundwork for officer material."

Service was compulsory at many public and Grammar schools in the late 1950s. Political expediency led to the abolition of conscription and the formation of the UK's first fully professional armed services. However, the ever-present threat of an escalation of the Cold War meant that reserve or territorial units had to be on constant standby for call-ups—what better way to bolster numbers than to provide basic military training to schoolchildren between twelve and eighteen? The consequences were that in the event of a sudden outbreak of hostilities, cadets would become the first drafted into service. Naturally, this minor but significant piece of information was never revealed to the pupils.

During the summer of 1961, I attended an infantry weaponry maintenance course at Bovington tank base in Dorset, and with the technical expertise acquired, I was promoted to school armourer. The armoury, a concrete breeze-block building, stood adjacent to the school bicycle shed and contained an indoor 25-yard rifle range, a collection of ageing First World War Lee Enfield '303' rifles, Sterling submachine guns, Bren light machine guns and enough ammunition to start a revolution in a banana republic. Security was a steel-plated door with a pair of rusty padlocks. It was baffling that no terrorist group short of weaponry ever attempted a break-in.

The armoury plan was simple. Two evenings a week after school, cadets had to report in full uniform for parade and inspection. Hours at home were spent bringing the kit up to scratch: belts and webbing were blancoed, boots polished, brass shined, and battle dress ironed. Only the armourer and his assistant were excused from the parade, so while everyone else spent the time square-bashing around the schoolyard, I passed the time drinking Coca-Cola and playing cards in the comfort of the armoury.

"Well, sir, I'm contemplating enrolling in a Fine Art course.

Mill's pasty complexion turned puce.

"College of Art? This country requires no more artists. Those parasites ferment social unrest and openly pursue immoral lifestyles. No boy will be permitted to tarnish this school's reputation. I will expect your application for a scholarship to Sandhurst on my desk by tomorrow!"

Many, including myself, were unaware that Mills received a generous bonus from the Ministry of Education for every pupil offered a scholarship at Oxford or Cambridge University or any of the military academies. We never spoke again. However, had I heeded his advice then, the road I chose would not have proved, forty years later, to be a cul-de-sac ending with a loss of liberty.

INITIATION

Over the years, the slow advance of the vine and creepers had concealed the eight-foot-high sandstone walls, built initially to discourage inquiring eyes. Beyond the imposing wrought-iron gates, a gravel road, overhung with chestnut and willow, snaked towards a forbidding Victorian manor house.

St. James Hospital was a permanent and temporary residence for one hundred and twenty psychiatric patients. I had been hired as a porter, a temporary job that would see me through the summer until the beginning of my first term at art college the following September 1964. Non-medical and menial duties involved moving supplies or patients back and forth within the complex. The 'uniform', a knee-length white linen coat, led to additional confusion amongst the already discombobulated patients who mistakenly referred to me as 'doctor.'

Most of the inmates were, however, under constant and heavy sedation, spending most of their days either staring endlessly into space or shuffling around the hospital grounds like zombies. The exception was Mrs. Roberts, a diminutive lady with a blue rinse, who twenty-four years earlier had tragically witnessed her husband's death during a German bombing raid. The trauma and shock had left her permanently scarred, believing, as she did, that

Britain had lost the war and was under German occupation. Anyone in any uniform was assumed to be a 'Geheime Statspolizei' (Gestapo) member.

On my second morning on the job, a fellow porter and I were dispatched to the geriatric ward to collect the body of an elderly female patient who had passed away during the night. Some years before, I had witnessed a body being fished out of Portsmouth Harbour, but I still felt squeamish at the thought of having to stretcher a corpse to the pathology laboratory.

The woman's body, frail and wasted by disease, felt light as a feather as we lifted it onto the marble examination table. We were about to take our leave when the pathologist asked if I wouldn't mind raising the dead woman's torso in an upright position. It was hardly a task to relish, but I wouldn't directly contact the cold flesh as I wore rubber gloves. When the woman's body reached an upright position, an enormous belch issued from her throat. A look of abject horror spread across my face. I instantly let go of my grip, and the woman's head fell backwards, hitting the marble with a dull thud. The pathologist began laughing uncontrollably.

"After all these years, it never fails."

As the newest staff recruit, I had undergone one of the hospital's curious initiation ceremonies.

The only bonus to date from working at the hospital was the female nursing staff, and I struck up a relationship with a twenty-two-year-old psychiatric nurse named Susan. She enjoyed my sense of humour, which lifted her spirits from the depression of her duties, and we started seeing one another socially. One evening, after a drink at our local pub, Susan invited me back to her flat for a nightcap. In her spare time, she wrote poetry and felt that I was sufficiently sensitive to share in the intimacy of her writing. She insisted that I read her verse out loud whilst she knelt and listened attentively at my feet. The request seemed somewhat bizarre, but after a few minutes of labouring over the poorly composed material, I suddenly felt Susan's hand opening my trouser zip.

"Don't stop. Don't let me interrupt you." She pleaded.

I continued to read aloud as her hand began caressing my groin. I glanced downward as her lips engulfed the head of my penis. I was about to receive my first experience of fellatio. The following morning, the other on-duty hospital staff member commented on my high spirits. There was a collective outburst of laughter when I revealed I had spent the evening at Susan's apartment. The other on-duty hospital porters commented on my high spirits. There was a collective outburst of laughter when I revealed I had spent the evening at Susan's apartment.

"How was the poetry reading?"

Professionally, Susan had become fascinated by a new revolutionary form of therapy recently introduced as an adjunct to the treatment of acute alcoholism and schizophrenia. A fresh range of 'chemotherapy' involving the experimental drug LSD had superseded electric shock and other outdated treatments. However, the drug had not yet received universal approval within the medical community. Nevertheless, initial results were encouraging, and enthusiasm grew for its use in various disorders.

As part of the ongoing research, Susan had been administered, under controlled conditions, a low dosage of the drug. Her experience had been a true revelation, believing as she did that her creative skills had been enhanced, although if her poetry was anything to go by, there was no clear evidence. She was convinced that as someone who was about to enter Art school, I could benefit enormously from a similar encounter with the drug. Under peer pressure and the desire to continue our poetry reading soirees, I agreed to undergo, with her mentorship and guidance, an LSD-induced session.

As a child, I had always shunned medication and, into my early teenage years, still refused to take aspirin for a common headache. I was seventeen, didn't smoke and now, with my brain between my thighs, I was about to put into my system a mysterious chemical that even the medical authorities had not fully sanctioned. I posed all the obvious negative questions: "Was it dangerous? Was it life-threatening, or could one suffer permanent brain damage? Could I end up as a patient in this very hospital?" I was reassured that as long as I maintained a positive outlook, then all the pleasurable thoughts and feelings would become exquisite, alluring, seductive and sensual. I was convinced that I could look forward to the mother of all blowjobs, but little did I imagine that over the next few hours, sex would be one of the last things on my mind.

A faint offshore breeze took the edge off the stiflingly hot June afternoon. We sat in the shade of a chestnut tree's bough, gazing towards the circular islands of flowerbeds protruding from the manicured hospital grounds. Susan handed me a glass ampoule from her apron pocket containing a colourless liquid. Its label read.

LSD 25

DELYSID

200µg

25ml. Aqueous solution

SANDOZ

I snapped the cap, held my breath, glanced tentatively at Susan and, anticipating some ghastly medicinal taste, poured the contents directly down my throat. Apart from a slight metallic tang, the liquid was remarkably tasteless. We sat chatting, Susan calming and reassuring me of my safety. Fifteen minutes passed, then twenty. I had begun to relax, but no other apparent physiological change occurred. I was convinced nothing would happen when I noticed I was losing track of the conversations. Susan's speech began reverberating as if she were talking through a megaphone in an echo chamber, and she was barely six inches from my face. I stared at the grass that was beginning to sway rhythmically. I glanced at the foliage on a nearby oozing tree and flowing green lava. Visually, everything was becoming a state of constant flux. Colours were vivid, luminescent like fauna on a coral reef brushed by an ocean current. The hairs on the back of my hand were swaying to and fro. The outline of Susan's form was becoming indistinct. I was drawn to the flowerbeds by the brilliance of the blossoms. I could see a pink rose breathing. The entire floral array appeared as a vast futuristic metropolis inhabited by a strange entomological civilisation. I sat cross-legged, staring, bewildered, mesmerised by this alien hive of industry. There were sudden dark moments of fear when I believed I had lost touch with reality forever, but Susan was there, squeezing my hand and offering comfort and support.

When the effects of the drug began to recede, I believed that only an hour had elapsed since I swallowed the liquid, but six hours had passed. I had lost track of time. That night, I stayed with Susan and awoke the following morning having slept like a baby. I felt refreshed and with a remarkable clarity of mind. What exactly was this potent compound that I had ingested? The amount consumed had been less than two hundred millionths of a gram, practically invisible to the naked eye and yet its effects had been so overwhelming and dramatic.

The year was 1938, and the dark cloud of Hitler and Nazism was descending over central Europe. Following Neville Chamberlain's failed appeasement, German troops had marched unopposed into Prague whilst Switzerland, with its fragile neutrality, struggled to remain oblivious to the turmoil beginning to engulf states surrounding her borders.

In Basel, at the Sandoz pharmaceutical company, a thirty-two-year-old chemist, Albert Hofmann, was immersed in studying ergot, a rye fungus. This strange substance was presumed to have far-reaching pharmacological properties, and Hofmann had already isolated and synthesised several promising compounds. The twenty-fifth in the series, lysergic acid diethylamide had been appropriately labelled and filed as LSD-25. Subsequent testing proved inconclusive, and the vial of LSD-25 was left to gather dust. It would be five years before the chemist would return and re-evaluate the compound.

"A strange feeling" had led Hofmann to produce a fresh batch. On April 16th, 1943, having completed the synthesis, it appears that the chemist probably accidentally absorbed the drug into his system through a small cut in his finger. Within a short period, he was overwhelmed by:

"I experienced a remarkable but not unpleasant state of intoxication characterised by intense stimulation of the imagination and an altered state of awareness of the world. As I lay in a dazed condition with my eyes closed, a succession of fantastic, rapidly changing imagery of striking reality and depth surged up from me, alternating with a vivid, kaleidoscopic play of colours. This condition passed after about three hours."

Hofmann could not understand how a sufficient amount of LSD-25 had passed into his body unnoticed, let alone comprehend the bizarre nature of the experiences he had encountered.

Three as later on April 19th. He conducted the first controlled LSD experiment on himself, ingesting two hundred and fifty microns, roughly equivalent to a hundred-thousandth of an ounce. He believed that swallowing such a minuscule dosage would have an almost negligible effect, and, therefore, he would be unrestricted in monitoring and analysing the results. As in Mary Shelley's "Frankenstein", LSD was about to bite back its creator. Bicycling home with his laboratory assistant, the effects were far more potent than he could have possibly anticipated.

"I had great difficulty in speaking coherently. My field of vision swayed before me, and objects appeared distorted like images in a curved mirror. I was unable to move from the spot, although my assistant told me afterwards that we had cycled at a good pace."

In 1942, the United States government established the Office of Strategic Services (OSS) to coordinate intelligence gathering and anticipate the probable outbreak of war. Under Colonel William Donovan's aegis, this newly formed agency embarked on a covert research programme into the development of 'truth serums.'

Would it be possible to interrogate and deprogram captured foreign espionage agents by merely administering into their systems a potent dose of a truth drug? The Nazis had successfully employed such compounds experimentally on innocent victims in concentration camps, and details of their work had leaked to the Allies. The Second World War ended, and the OSS was restructured and transformed into the Central Intelligence Agency (CIA).

The advent of the Cold War led to an expansion of American research projects in the field of mind control and chemical interrogation methods. The services of academics, psychiatrists and hypnotists were integrated into the programme under the code name "Bluebird." Finance for the project was funnelled through secret slush funds, and the research was one of the agency's most closely guarded secrets. It wasn't long before the CIA got wind of a hallucinatory substance under production at the Sandoz laboratory in Switzerland, and early in 1950, LSD entered the cornucopia of chemicals in the agency's arsenal. LSD provisionally proved unreliable as a truth serum, but the CIA was fascinated by the fact that such minute doses of the drug could bring on:

"Serious mental confusion and rendering the mind temporarily to suggestion."

Trials have shown that the effects could vary from euphoria to complete terror. Agency scientists could not envisage any practical application for LSD. Still, concern spread when it was realised that copious amounts of ergotamine tartrate, the precursor for the synthesis of the drug, were readily available within the communist bloc. The Sandoz laboratory was still the world's sole producer of LSD, and only relatively small amounts of the drug were available worldwide to researchers. When a CIA operative in Bulgaria intercepted a Chinese intelligence signal revealing the impending purchase of the drug, panic broke out in Washington, DC. Unfortunately, in his excitement, the agent misread the message, interpreting it as a request to procure 1000 grams of Lysergide, enough to make 100 million doses. The amount was merely a milligram or the equivalent of 10 doses, but the die was cast. The Central Intelligence Agency set about the procurement of all available supplies of LSD and ergotamine tartrate.

In 1953, the then director of the CIA, Allen Dulles, authorised Richard Helms, the head of his clandestine services section, to push ahead with a significant mind-control project codenamed MK-ULTRA. The programme ran unabated for the next ten years, and ordinary American citizens from all walks of life became unwitting guinea pigs. Target victims were initially drawn from society's deprived underbelly. Penal inmates, people with mental health conditions, ethnic minorities and individuals suffering from terminal illnesses were easy pickings for the CIA.

As research advanced, the intelligence community even fooled around with one another, spiking fellow agents' drinks at parties and social gatherings. Brothels fronted safe houses where unsuspecting customers were dosed and observed through two-way mirrors. Even dopers and junkies were rounded up and invited to LSD 'acid' parties where agents monitored their ensuing behaviour. The concept of spiking whole city water supplies or releasing the drug through an urban population in aerosol form was even considered as a possible future covert psycho-chemical weapon. LSD's use as a tool of political assassination was contemplated, and it is widely believed that the drug was employed in one of the many failed attempts on the life of the Cuban Marxist leader Fidel Castro.

Despite the CIA's evil intentions, the psychiatric community had embraced LSD as a tool in several experimental therapies for numerous medical disorders. As an adjunct to psychoanalysis, low-dose techniques were practised in clinics throughout Western

Europe, whilst, in Canada, high-dose treatments of alcoholic disorders were proving remarkably successful. Much of the pioneering work with the drug was ongoing in mental institutions in the United Kingdom.

GETTING HIGHER EDUCATION

Moving from Grammar school to Art college, I felt like a monk who had recanted his vows: no timetable, no dress code, no higher authority and a plethora of women. The term's opening week started with a bang with the 'Freshman's Ball.' The first social event of the college calendar. The Art school, with only two hundred students and a limited budget, would combine its resources with Portsmouth's College of Technology, thus enabling more lavish productions to be staged.

Beatlemania was sweeping the country, but in the south of England, the raw R&B sound of the Rolling Stones and John Mayall's blues breakers had a core following, especially amongst the student community. The ball was held at the indoor theatre of the city's South Parade Pier. This Victorian seafront edifice sadly suffered irreparable damage a few years later during the shooting of Ken Russell's film version of The Who's rock opera 'Tommy.' Regrettably, the evening turned into a personal disaster. Whilst endeavouring to impress and charm a red-haired sculpture student, I underestimated the strength of the scrumpy, cloudy concoction from the bottom of the cider barrel. I spent most of the night bent over a toilet bowl. It is a pity that I failed to make a good impression on the redhead and missed live performances by the legendary American blues artists Muddy Waters, Sonny Terry and Brownie McGhee. However, in a rare moment of cognisance, I caught an electrifying set by an u-and-coming English guitarist and former art student, Eric 'Slow Hand.' Clapton and his band The Yardbirds.

I joined the college film society, and for the first time, I saw works by acclaimed international directors. Films from luminaries such as

Akira Kurosawa, Jean-Luc Godard, and Ingmar Bergman were true revelations. The society's philosophy was catholic, with classic Westerns and Ealing comedies often featured alongside more arty productions. Nevertheless, outside of college, live music was my greatest passion, and I took every opportunity to catch performances by the new wave of English musicians and bands.

The college's local pub was the 'Raven', and once a week, I took over the upstairs function room, where I would spin a selection of Motown and soul music using a scratchy P.A. system. The evening, I built up a cult following as a regular venue where students would hang out and, unheeded, openly smoke hashish. The Thursday night event became so popular that scores of young people had to be turned away each week. The landlord, Karl, an affable Dane who had led the Danish resistance movement against the Nazis in the Second World War, turned a blind eye to the dubious upstairs activities as the overspill invariably ended up drinking downstairs in the pub.

The academic side of my studies could best be described as flexible, as I rarely attended on-campus the first year. The broad-based curriculum embraced all aspects of Art & Design. At the end of the first year, students select a specialised course of study that they will pursue for the three remaining years of their degree. The options available ranged from Fine Art: painting, sculpture, and printmaking to Film & television and graphic design: fashion and Jewellery. Londo colleges traditionally had the kudos, but in the field of painting, they were woefully lacking in facilities. Painters endured physical restrictions and often found themselves crammed into shoe-box-sized studio spaces.

Although Portsmouth suffered from its provinciality, the Art school's reputation had grown Several leading British artists rapidly visited and lectured in the Fine Art department. The school building had been designed and purpose-built as an art facility in the early 1960s. Studios were high-ceilinged warehouse-sized spaces, glass-fronted on two sides, and with only sixteen students for each academic year, the ratio of students to studio space was two to one.

As a vibrant international metropolis, London had much to offer, but from my standpoint, The city had an up-and-coming music scene and the bonus of the beach and sea in the summer.

I grew my hair long, wore faded paint-stained jeans-shirts and sneakers and after further failed attempts at drinking booze, began smoking hash recreationally. Following the success of the nights at the 'Raven', I took up the Student Union Social Secretary post, with painting taking a back seat for the next couple of years. There was 'compulsory' attendance at Art History and Psychology of Art seminars where, despite my numerous 'no-shows', I somehow managed to keep abreast of my studies.

Will Clark taught psychology classes. Later, at the age of forty-eight, he was drawn to higher education. He majored in anthropology and, after completing a thesis on the ancient cultures of Mesoamerica, was awarded a doctorate. Then, in his mid-fifties, it was mystifying to find him stuck out in the sticks teaching the psychology of art.

Will was an avid and hypnotic storyteller who kept students engrossed with accounts of his travels throughout Mexico and Central America. His particular field of interest lay in the shamanic influences and the ritual and ceremonial use of plants and herbs in tribal sacraments. I found his accounts of encounters and experimentation with, in particular, psilocybin, peyote and yage engrossing. He was the first person I had met with first-hand experiences of organic psychedelics. He constantly referred to his beliefs of alternative realities and the eternal search for the inner self. Course reading was unsurprisingly Aldous Huxley's "Doors of Perception" and R.D. Laing's "Politics of Ecstasy."

Having previously shared with Will my impressions of the LSD experience, He invited me to join four other students to undergo a monitored LSD experiment at a weekend country retreat. There were no observers in white coats but, on the contrary, an atmosphere of friendliness and ease in a picturesque rural setting. We weren't required to perform any convoluted physical tests, paint, draw or attempt any written record whilst under the influence of the drug. I guess the fundamental aim was to consider any post-high creative enhancement; where my first LSD 'trip' had been primarily a visual exploration, this journey turned into an audio voyage.

From the chill of the garden and just before the drug began to take effect, I hastened indoors and sat cross-legged in front of a blazing fire. A Miles Davis album was playing through the stereo. I closed my eyes, and a kaleidoscope of vibrating colours immediately danced harmoniously with the music. Suddenly, jazz, as an abstract music form, began to make complete sense to me. I was hooked by a style of music I had previously found incomprehensible. The following day, I trailed from one second-hand record store to another, snapping up the music of Coltrane, Charlie Parker and other jazz luminaries.

Before the weekend, Chris Adams, a Yorkshire lad, had spent his studio time churning out an uninspired series of drab and sombre landscapes, with his palette ranging from off-white, murky browns and greys to black. Perhaps his work's bleakness reflected his Northern village background, but sadly, their only redeeming feature was the ornate frames that encased his work. Within three days of his psychedelic initiation, Chris could be seen working enthusiastically, painting panoramic vistas of giant garish blades of grass. He claimed that having wandered into the garden during his LSD trip, he had become disorientated and found himself in a sea of multi-coloured pastures. The experience had inspired the direction his new work had taken him. It made complete sense to me, although I am not sure he hadn't already derailed from the given path to this day. Regardless, for the next two years, he seemed perfectly comfortable endlessly painting blades of grass.

Although my own painting's output was barely reaching the requirement, it took on a more abstract geometrical style. This was due primarily to my duties as the college social secretary, which took up more of my time than anticipated. I had initially selected sculpture as an ancillary subject, but I switched to printmaking as a medium as it best suited the development of my artwork. This was a fortuitous decision that was to greatly impact my work in years to come.

As the summer term of 1966 ended, I travelled to Sweden in search of the delights of Scandinavian' free love', accompanied by fellow student Roger 'Arnie' Palmer, who spent more time on a golf course than in class. Our research proved rewarding and time-consuming. We took some time out to watch the football World Cup final between England and Germany in a student hostel. The room was full of raucous Germans, who graciously insisted on buying the two of us celebratory drinks after the match. It wasn't long before I was back on my knees in the bathroom!

I returned to college earlier to work on the planning and organisation of the forthcoming. Freshman's ball. The main student body was due in two weeks, with the annual extravaganza set for the following weekend. Upon arrival, the entire Student Union committee, of which I was a member, was summoned to an urgent meeting in the principal's office. In attendance were two officials, purportedly from the Home Office—their brief concerns about the increase nationally of left-wing dissident student movements. The proclamation outlined a programme to clamp down nationally on such activities. In addition, this embraced a campaign aimed at addressing the increase in illicit drug use throughout the student community. Effectively, we were asked as responsible committee members to grass on fellow students engaging in anti-social behaviour. I glanced across the room at the union president, who attended the LSD weekend and now supplemented his student grant by dealing hash. Accepting such a directive would mean virtually the entire student body, and most staff would be under investigation. An outcome none of the committee were willing to pursue.

Finals were a year away, and I hadn't made any appreciable progress with my painting or printmaking. In addition to building up a portfolio of work for an exhibition, I had to write a five-thousand-word thesis. I figured I could assemble the artwork in the final few months. Still, because of my thesis, I spent the summer of 1967 researching three relatively unknown American contemporary artists.

Frank Stella, Jules Olitski and Kenneth Noland were pioneers in the field of post-painterly abstraction. A style that focused on flat painted surfaces utilizing bright, vivid colours in a linear format. Their interest in the psychology of colour dovetailed with my own, and it was exciting to exchange views and opinions with the two leading painters of this blossoming art movement who were part of the new American avant-garde, a movement coined 'Post Painterly Abstractionism.' A title that was as pseudo-intellectual as the Californian art historian Clement Greenberg, who had initially penned it. I had a genuine interest in their work, but there was also a clear strategy in choosing to write about these particular artists. The Movement was still in its infancy, and I surmised there was very little chance that anyone in the UK would be aware of the group's existence. The odds of any degree assessor's familiarity with either artist were extremely low. Therefore, I naturally presumed it would be tough, if not impossible, to evaluate my thesis critically. I would pass with flying colours as long as it was well-written, legible, and presentable.

I travelled over the summer to the United States, where I had the opportunity to speak with two of the artists in question. I finished the printed and bound tome a week before the start of the Autumn term and spent the next six months rattling off numerous silk-screen and lithographic print editions. I completed a half dozen large format paintings and filled a sizable portfolio with drawings and designs. Most of the remaining time before finals was spent on the beach, cramming my brain with the art history curriculum.

My degree adjudicators judged my painting to 'lack depth.' and that I seemed overly concerned with the production of artefacts. Had I missed something, or wasn't that the object of the exercise? How else do you stage an exhibition? I scrapped a BA degree in Fine Art in June 1967 and gathered with fellow graduates and staff members for the perfunctory celebration 'piss up' across the road at the 'Raven.'

Before relocating to Portsmouth to study sculpture, Bill Foulkes, an 'exiled' Liverpudlian,

He lived with his two elder brothers on the Isle of Wight for several years. In the three years since we had known one another, I had never seen Bill dressed in a filthy white T-shirt, navy blue pinstripe suit, and white plimsolls. A cigarette dangled perpetually from his mouth. He was a creature of the night, spontaneous and reckless. Following one of our regular Thursday night social gatherings, he and I, on the spur of the moment, drove through the night to Liverpool. For no particular reason, although I like to think Bill suddenly became homesick. Arriving early the following morning, we grabbed breakfast and drove back to Portsmouth. Bill always seemed to live life on the throw of the dice.

"Got any plans for the summer?" I asked.

"Plans?" He looked bewildered.

"I might get involved with Ronnie and Ray's music festival on the island."

The two elder brothers had become involved in a fund-raising project for the Isle of Wight Swimming Pool Association. I was curious to know more about the festival. Bill was a bit vague, but it was supposed to be a rock and roll event, and according to him, the brothers had booked it:

"Somebody called the Jefferson Airplane?"

I choked briefly on my drink.

Although still relatively unknown outside of the United States, Jefferson Airplane was already one of America's most successful new-wave rock bands, playing a style of music that was later to be labelled psychedelic. I prided myself on having my finger on the music pulse at that time. Still, I had no idea the band was visiting

England, let alone performing on the Isle of Wight for a local charity organization. This seemed highly improbable.

"Are you sure you've got the band's name right, Bill?"

The contracts had been signed weeks before; amazingly, everything was set for August.

Well, I say everything was set, but the reality at that time was that Ronnie and Ray Foulkes had lined up a field for the 'festival' site but hadn't yet got around to any advertising or promotion. There had been no mention of the event in the music press, and the event was due to take place in less than eight weeks.

The following day, after volunteering my services to the brothers, I travelled by hovercraft to Cowes on the Isle of Wight. There, I was greeted by the brothers and driven to the Foulke family residence, a gothic 'gingerbread' house on the west coast village of Freshwater.

How had these two amiable but ditzy brothers booked one of the world's leading rock bands from their backwater island retreat? I quizzed them on the status of their preparations only to discover that their efforts to date amounted to a £100 rental deposit on a wheat field and a newly published two-inch advert in the national music weekly 'Melody Maker.' The Move, Tyrannosaurus Rex, Fairport Convention, the Crazy World of Arthur Brown and other acts had been added to the rostrum, the event to be held over the August Bank Holiday weekend. No staging, fencing or amenities had been arranged, and on inspection, the uncut wheat field was nearly three feet high. No electrical generators were booked, no portable toilets were available, and all of the island's available bus and coach transportation had been reserved in advance of the holiday weekend.

If the Airplane's management learned of the shambolic situation, it was a distinct possibility that they would cancel their appearance. Someone with credibility and influence would have to be brought on board to reassure music business agents in London that the festival was a bona fide event and would be handled professionally.

Portsmouth's 'Birdcage' nightclub was one of those acoustically perfect low-ceilinged venues.

The place I imagined resembled a 1930s Chicago speakeasy—an intimate but seedy establishment. A well-known London impresario named Rikki Farr had taken over the club's management, enabling the 'Birdcage' to showcase numerous headline acts.

Following the club's recent renovation, the band 'The Who', whose notoriety preceded them, had taken to the stage. After two hours of blistering sonic bombardment, the band demolished the newly installed state-of-the-art lighting system and their instruments. I returned to the mainland and headed straight to the nightclub, expecting to be greeted by Rikki. In the interim, the club had changed its name to 'Brave New World', and instead of meeting Rikki, Farr was confronted by a man in his early twenties dressed from head-to-toe in matching brown shirt, brown trousers, knee-high polished jackboots and sporting a Nazi swastika armband. Unbeknown the club had changed hands earlier that week.

And standing before me was the spectre of the new owner, Nicholas Hoogstraten.

Soon by deed poll to become 'Van' Hoogstraten, he was to acquire early notoriety a few months later when arrested for tossing a hand grenade into the front garden of a Brighton rabbi. He later became one of Britain's most reviled slum landlords.

I finally met Rikki Farr at his apartment and briefed him on the potential fiasco for the Isle of Wight. Ricki was one of those charismatic figures who could convert a sceptic in minutes. Notwithstanding a substantial amount of bullshit, he could talk a glass eye to sleep!

After several urgent phone calls to London, it was soon revealed that the Foulke brothers had already reneged on their contractual obligations with several bands by failing to pay advances on time. When I returned to the island, Rikki's influence calmed the doubters.

Ronnie and Ray Foulkes had played the festival charity card for all it was worth. There was hardly any capital available for even basic set-up costs. Lines of credit and loans were often acquired through bartering and, in some cases, coercion. Students from the Art college were enlisted to design and print posters and tickets, whilst farm workers were press-ganged into cutting the wheat field, erecting fencing and constructing a sound stage. Wives, relatives and friends kept the motley crew's batteries recharged with sandwiches and gallons of brewed tea, and the whole project began to take on a life of its own.

Visiting the Isle of Wight was like stepping back in time. After a six-mile sea crossing, you felt like you had arrived in pre-World War 11 England. The unfortunate islanders had no idea what was about to infiltrate and erode their tranquillity and isolationism.

The advertisement in the Melody Maker had unexpectedly attracted numerous inquiries, and a week before the festival was due to take place, a small, tented village had mushroomed on the outskirts of the site. Short of the workforce, the Foulkes had offered early arrivals free festival entrance in exchange for their labour on the construction site.

Located ten miles east of Ryde and the ferry terminals and with no direct public bus service, there were still no plans for transporting festival goers to the site. Worst still, the island car ferry service was booked solidly over the holiday weekend. Fortunately, the daughter of the ferry service's managing director had purchased tickets for the festival and sensed an opportunity to pad the company's revenue; her father quickly recommissioned from mothballing an ancient paddle steamer, which was requisitioned for festival attendees. I managed to block-book the fledgling island hovercraft service to transport the artists from and to the mainland, paying in full in advance with a check that, if cashed that day, would have bounced to the moon and back. An estimated 18,000 tickets needed to be sold to break even, but barely a week prior, less than half had been sold. A dark cloud of financial gloom descended.

Considering the chaos that reigned, it was hardly surprising that no decision had yet been made.

They reached out regarding the event's food concessions. Thousands of partygoers and hippies weren't necessarily bringing Fortnum & Mason food hampers; the nearest supermarket and grocery store was at least seven miles away. Forty-eight hours before the weekend, we bought up every burger, hot dog and soft drink we could find, and all other food concessionaires were banned from the site. By Friday afternoon, a full day before the main event began, the festival crowd had swollen to 5000. That evening, local bands and street entertainers gave impromptu performances. A giant village fete atmosphere was starting to evolve and unfold.

On Saturday morning, I journeyed to the mainland by hovercraft to await and coordinate the arrival of the musicians and their entourages. I returned to the island just after 6 pm in the company of the headline act, the Jefferson Airplane. We boarded a dilapidated coach and set off from the terminal. The interior of the vehicle quickly became engulfed in a dense cloud of sweet marijuana fumes. Joints of high-grade weed were passing back and forth. These native Californians had arrived well-prepared, but mild paranoia overcame me, and I feared for the well-being of the bus driver. My concerns were interrupted by fits of uncontrollable laughter. I felt utterly comatose. How could the band members possibly perform in this state?

After what seemed like an eternity, the bus finally drew to a halt. I stumbled out just as the 'Crazy World of Arthur Brown' was performing their rendition of the Fire anthem. A crane lowered the weird-looking Arthur onto the stage, his head capped in a flaming headdress and face daubed in fluorescent paint—an exciting entrance. Arthur's antics and pyrotechnics bemused the American entourage, but the crowd lapped the spectacle.

Ricki Farr emceed the evening show, and the headlining Jefferson Airplane took to the stage around midnight. There were renditions of their classic songs 'White Rabbit' and 'Somebody to Love', but overall, the performance lacked a real spark. Too much dope, perhaps?

Over the following day, the 19,000-odd satisfied paying customers and several thousand freebies dispersed and headed home. The Isle of Wight Swimming Pool Association received enough money to lay the foundations of the building project. With a slice from the food sales, I could afford not to have to join the dole queue in the foreseeable future. The pioneering event was to put the Isle of Wight on the world map, leading as it did the following two years to massive festival events and the establishment of a music festival tradition that has continued to this day. I joined Jefferson Airplane at their final British gig at London's Roundhouse the following weekend—an all-night doubleheader with their West Coast compatriots, 'The Doors.

UMBILICAL DISCORD

The Roundhouse in Chalk Farm, North London, had started life as a railway locomotive maintenance shed. Still, in the early 1960s and subject to the government's nationalisation programme, the facility became surplus to requirement. The local Camden Council, who owned the land that the building stood on, inherited the property; however, without any apparent practical use and no investment, the circular landmark fell into disuse. With very few venues available for 'progressive' rock music in London, a group of enterprising promoters took up an option on the Roundhouse. The bleak, soot-stained interior was transformed into a Mecca of underground music from Friday night to Sunday morning. Christened 'Middle Earth' for the occasion, 'Op Art' banners were hung, and an in-the-round psychedelic light show augmented gigs by such groundbreaking bands as Soft Machine and Pink Floyd. Market stalls sold clothing, vinyl records, hippie paraphernalia, and a macrobiotic food stand, which provided sustenance for all-night revellers. Virtually all those in attendance had their stash of Red Lebanese, Indian Temple Balls, Pakistani Chitral or Afghani hashish, The sweet odour of which permeated the interior.

Each Sunday at 6 am, the festivities closed, and everyone headed home in a reasonably orderly fashion. There wa no rowdiness or disturbances, and everyone showed respect for the neighborhood residents. Sunglasses were considered a necessity and an essential fashion accessory during those early hours. Revellers who were still not ready for bed would cross the road to 'Marine Ices', where they could satisfy the drug-induced munchies. "Anyone for Sicilian Cassata or a chocolate bombe?"

The early sight of dozens of long-haired, drug-fuelled freaks dressed in an assortment of Kaftans, military jackets, and other ethnic attire must have been a severe culture shock for the staff of the family-run Italian ice cream parlour.

I had an invitation to meet up with the Airplane band members earlier in the afternoon before the Roundhouse concert. We ate lunch at the pre-Hard Rock Cafe hamburger joint, 'The Great American Disaster'; fingers are crossed this wasn't a bad omen for the evening show. A casual conversation with the guitarist Paul Kantner led him to ask if I'd heard of LSD. He seemed genuinely surprised to hear that a provincial Englishman had come across the drug four years earlier and had tried it on more than one occasion. From the inside pocket of his embroidered waistcoat, he removed a small brown aspirin bottle from which he poured into his hand two pills, passing them across to me. They were samples of 'Orange Sunshine,' the first mass-produced illicit LSD.

A shady bunch of surfing dopers from Orange County in Southern California who had been running a methamphetamine operation in Laguna Beach had become converts to LSD. Over the next three years, the 'Brotherhood of Love' flooded the market with the potent 'Orange Sunshine' controlling virtually the entire illicit supply of LSD in the United States.

The 500+ micron acid was much stronger than my previous experiences. I also elected to take it before the show that night, so it was to be my first 'night trip.' The audio and visual hallucinations I began to experience distorted my senses to such an extent that I could no longer distinguish the musicians or their music. At least the Doors and the Airplane performed on two consecutive nights, so on the second evening, I got to see and listen under normal circumstances.

My final act as Art College Social Secretary was to stage the end-of-term dance at South Parade Pier. I approached Island Records with a proposal for the company featuring artists solely from their record label. The band's Traffic, Spooky Tooth and Free were offered to the college at a reduced fee, and Island Records was prepared to subsidise a portion of the promotional costs. Two thousand punters attended the show at the outdoor auditorium on a balmy June evening. The event proved a great success, and the record company was more than satisfied with their acts' exposure.

After the Roundhouse weekend of temporary insanity, I remained in London for a few days. On a whim, I paid a social visit to Island Records at their office on Oxford Street in the West End. The company occupied the second floor of the building, sandwiched between the music impresario Micky Most and the embryonic Chrysalis Records. The independent company functioned as an extended family, with management, agency, A & R, and art departments all coordinated under one roof. Operating in a niche market in the late 1960s, the label dabbled with psychedelic rock bands before its founder, Chris Blackwell, drawing on his West Indian music heritage, was to bring Bob Marley to the world's attention.

I was greeted at reception by Alec Leslie, with whom I had liaised when setting up the island south-coast promotion, ushered into the office and introduced to Johnny Glover, Alec's partner and the A & R director, Muff Winwood. Hailing from Birmingham, Muff had played bass guitar in the Spencer Davis Group, fronted by his younger brother Steve. Tired of touring, newly married and having a mortgaged house in Pinner, Middlesex, Muff had stepped back behind the scenes and into Island Records. His short hair, suit and tie seemed inconsistent with his previous employment. Previously, his name had been suggested as a possible choice of bass player for a new supergroup, Blind Faith, featuring his brother, Eric Clapton and drummer Ginger Baker. However, it's believed that his abstention from drug-taking may have eliminated him from the shortlist. Muff proved to be a man of integrity and a highly successful A & R expert, and I was surprised but delighted to receive an offer of a position with the company. My role was never clearly defined, but I began work in the promotion department and ended in A & R, artist and repertory, seeking new talent to add to the label's blossoming reputation. There were some successes and a few failures. The young R&B group,' Free', and the eclectic 'King Crimson' were signed to the label. Still, the company passed over a bespectacled piano-player-singer-songwriter who failed to arouse any interest then. Island's rebuff appears to have had no noticeable effect on Elton John's long-term career. In A & R, one tends to keep anti-social hours. Endless nights he was often spent in dark, smoke-filled nightclubs waiting to hear some obscure act that the office receptionist's brother-in-law believes is the next Beatles. When the band finally takes to the stage, and their instruments are out of tune, you take your leave and head to the next venue.

The standard operating procedure for a pre-release record promotion was to hire a small, intimate venue, lay on a buffet, inexhaustible supplies of alcohol and invite the entire music press and friends from within the recording industry. These incestuous gatherings came around at alarming regularity and were invariably major binges, resulting in a high rate of absenteeism the following day. Island's promotions were always viewed as special events where Chris Blackwell would oversee blending his famous Jamaican punch. On a 'Traffic' forthcoming album release, the trendy Mayfair nightclub, the Revolution, was the location for the promo party. /By six-thirty evening, the venue was packed with the usual suspects. Cocktail servers in skimpy costumes served canapes and replenished drinks as the guests mingled and exchanged shoptalk. Band members wandered around, giving the occasional impromptu press interview. Slowly but surely, everyone became inebriated as copious amounts of homemade punch were consumed and replenished. The band planned to take the stage and give a cameo performance of the new releases, invariably receiving rapturous applause. At least, that was the intention. The problem on this occasion was everyone present was unaware that the band's road manager, the mischievous Albert, had laced Chris Blackwell's legendary 'Jamaican punch with liquid LSD. The net result was chaotic. Grown men in suits could be seen weeping and crawling on all fours. Others tried vainly to converse while several guests were seen talking to the wall. Incoherent band members could not locate their instruments, let alone play, and the club's management was forced to lock the doors from the inside to prevent anyone from leaving. Having elected to stick to red wine, I was one of the few who avoided an unforeseen state of psychosis. I really can't sanction spiking unwitting victims in this way. There is always someone who suffers, and in some cases, there is the risk of long-term psychological harm.

Island records continued to grow into a more prominent 'family' concern where many staff were recruited through 'bloodline. Friends would be added to the payroll without prior consideration for experience or ability. Unfortunately, this happy family began to marginalise the very individuals who were responsible for the company's wealth: the artists and musicians. The music business will always have many creative people, but most are not found in record companies. In February 1969, after an all too brief spell, I parted with the recording industry, vowing never to return.

MIDNIGHT SEXPRESS

Winter is not the ideal time to visit Sweden, but I had two months to kill before heading off to the Greek island of Paxos, where I planned to spend the summer at a friend's villa. Another ex-art school friend was similarly at a loose end, so he joined me. We set sail from the Lincolnshire port of Immingham bound for Gothenburg. The North Sea is a barren stretch of water at the best of times, but that night lingers long in the memory as one of the worst sea crossings I had ever undertaken. The night air was filled with the passengers' screams of terror as the ship was tossed about in a force-ten gale.

The following morning, a little after sunrise, I stumbled into the shipboard cafeteria to put something back into my stomach. The eatery resembled a scene from the 'Mary Celeste.' Scattered across the tables were a few half-eaten breakfasts but not a living soul in sight. The dining area would be packed on a calm crossing, but the room was eerily quiet that morning. A leaden sky greeted our disembarkment. The streets were carpeted in a discoloured coating of compacted snow lying where it had fallen three months earlier. Locals huddled together in their Winter wear. The entire landscape had had the colour sucked out of it. The buildings were grey, and people's faces were ashen. Unlike my summer visit to Sweden, the landscape was bare and denuded. I was already yearning for April and the waters of the Mediterranean. Perhaps this trip was a bad idea after all?

A Swedish companion I had met onboard during the crossing alerted me to the headline of the local newspaper, which he duly translated:

"FURTHER SEX VICTIMS SEIZED BY GIRL GANG"

A group of frustrated women had continued to prey on unsuspecting males in the suburb of Vastra Frolunda. Victims had been dragged to the woods and forced to have sexual intercourse with their abductors. A week later, under different circumstances, I was to meet the woman who was to become my wife. With hazelnut eyes and long brown hair, Eva was not your stereotypical Swede, but she turned her head wherever she went. It was love at first sight, and we became inseparable. All thoughts of a summer in Greece vanished from my mind. Unlike most Swedish city-dwellers, Eva's family migrated to the coast over the summer, where they owned a Sommarstuga or summer cottage. It was an isolated log cabin on the fringes of a pine forest, overlooking a coastal inlet dotted with blackened glass-smooth rock islets on which one could sunbathe naked into the late evening.

I signed up for an intensive Swedish language course at Gothenburg University. After three months of nothing but Swedish seven hours a day, six days a week, I became reasonably fluent. I supported myself by teaching English as a foreign language to native Swedes four nights a week at the British Institute and supplementing my income by DJing on the weekend at the city's only underground rock venue. This is hardly comparable to modern DJing, as there is no mixing involved.

"Lower the stylus onto the disc, preferably a Pink Floyd album, then head across the street to the park with friends to smoke hash. Return within thirty minutes and flip the record over."

Having maintained contact with some of the UK-based record companies, I regularly received advanced promotional material, much of which I reviewed in the local newspaper's music column. News from London would occasionally arrive through a good friend, David Gordon, who ran a wholesale clothing business that imported the latest UK fashion items.

On one of his monthly visits, he insisted I listen to a cassette of demo songs that his younger brother had written and recorded. Stephen had briefly flirted with the pop music business before being sidelined for a year with tuberculosis. Whilst convalescing, he had written a wonderful collection of charmingly innocent melodies, accompanying himself on either acoustic guitar or piano. The style bore minimal resemblance to his earlier recordings. He was currently without a recording contract, but an arranged meeting with my former employer, Chris Blackwell, and Island Records proved rewarding. Within two years, Cat Stevens was to become the most significant selling artist worldwide.

Along with the rest of the population, Eva and I endured the long, dark Swedish Winter months, yearning for those few magical weeks of summer when we could return to the summer cottage on the coast. Life in Sweden had become comfortable and routine but uneventful. Perhaps these feelings were a byproduct of the country's 'cradle to the grave' social welfare system, but I grew restless and longed for a change. However, I remained unwilling to break the umbilical cord of the facade of security with which I had surrounded myself. A proposition from David Gordon in early 1971 was to snap my complacency and isolationism.

Cat Stevens' career was at its height, and his success, fame, and wealth had grown proportionally. He had moved out of his Central London Shaftesbury Avenue flat, located above his father's restaurant, to a house in a fashionable part of West London. Uncertain of the advice he was receiving from his team of accountants, Steven had set up an independent property company with substantial funds available for investment.

By way of his brother, I had been offered the opportunity to return to London, take up residence in Steven's old flat, and David and I would go out and play' Monopoly' with real money.

The boy's father was well into his seventh decade, but age had not deterred the older man from continuing to operate his neighbourhood cafe seven days a week. Each morning, he would arrive punctually at six-thirty to open the doors for breakfast. The flat I now occupied was directly over the cafe whilst Ingrid, Steven and David's mother, divorced from their father, lived one floor above. The older man, formerly Mr. Georgiou, who had changed his name by proxy to Adams, had enjoyed a colourful life. Son of an impoverished shepherd on the island of Cyprus, he had sailed as a teenager to Egypt. He integrated himself into the sizeable Greek expat community of Alexandria, but with the political upheaval under the imperial rule of the British creating unrest in the country, he emigrated to the United States in the 1920s. During prohibition, he ran a speakeasy, but for reasons never made known and still holding British citizenship from his birthplace of Cyprus, he was deported to England shortly before the outbreak of World War 11. Now in London, he met and married Ingrid, a Swede, and together they raised three children: two sons, David and Steven and an elder daughter, Anita.

For some curious reason, the family disliked Georgiou's given name, which was only retained by his mother, Ingrid. In addition to the old man changing his name to Adams, David used the surname Gordon, Anita married a Bulgarian named Zolas, and Steven, presumably for professional reasons, changed his name to Cat Stevens. Since his conversion to Islam, he is now known as Yusuf Islam.

Each morning before setting off on our adventures in 'Property Investment, ' David and I would breakfast in the old man's cafe. Neither of us had a real grasp of the housing market, and Steven was always vague about his intentions. When asked, he would shrug his shoulders and respond,

"I don't know. Just go out and buy houses."

So, armed with a fat chequebook, we drove around London until something looked appealing.

Within weeks, we had purchased a half dozen residential properties, mainly around West London. Were we planning to rent or turn the properties around for a quick profit? Would we hoard bricks and mortar? Who knew? We certainly didn't. My suggestion that we roll a dice on an actual Monopoly board and buy up property in the corresponding area fell on deaf ears.

David and I continued traipsing the streets of London, but neither of us had our hearts in the property profession. He was living in what he perceived as his younger brother's shadow, which was increasingly becoming a personal issue. Not lacking in musical talent, he began to devote more of his time to songwriting, but the unavoidable comparison with his brother's music dented his confidence further.

With the release of his third album, 'Catch Bull at Four,' Steven's career was going from strength to strength, and he was soon to embark on a world tour. Live performances were an ordeal for Steven. Despite his meticulous preparations, he was constantly physically sick before going on stage. This nervous state brought him into constant conflict with his backing musicians, who found him very difficult to deal with.

In Steven's absence, David and I would file monthly progress reports with his management company, BKM. With no previous track record in the music business, the gregarious Barry Krost was an unusual choice as Steven's manager. A childhood actor, his roots were firmly embedded in the theatrical world, where he had risen to manage the likes of Peter Finch and playwright John Osborne. BKM's offices were located above the private club, the 'White Elephant' on Curzon Street, Mayfair, and are constantly awash with 'luvvies.' It seemed incongruous that Barry was now managing one of the world's leading pop stars.

Eva had settled into life in London and utilizing her linguistic skills had taken up a position with a translation company. With Steven's mother, Ingrid, living above us, she was still able to have regular chats in her native Swedish tongue.

ON THE ROAD AGAIN

Barry Krost's P.A. had more than just a soft spot for me, but despite his advances and sexual innuendo, he became resigned to my blatant heterosexuality. Nevertheless, he was always supportive and aware of my dissatisfaction with the house buying and arranged an interview with a music touring management company. I soon began working on the early planning of the Rolling Stones' proposed tour of Japan and Australia. Negotiations were completed, contracts were exchanged in the Autumn of 1972, and the tour was slated for early Spring the following year. The Japanese sector was slightly problematic as Keith Richards's alleged drug use and previous conviction were a hurdle yet to overcome. A bona fide medical certificate showing a clean bill of health was the first step, and Keith was packed off to Switzerland for a complete blood transfusion. This, it was hoped, would alleviate the Japanese authorities.

The Paul Dainty Organisation handled the Australian dates. The company had an excellent track record in that region and had handled Cat Stevens' Australasian leg of his recently completed world tour. My logistics manager's responsibility was coordinating the tour's travel and accommodation details. In total, there were to be approximately sixty people in the touring party who would be arriving from various parts of the planet in Sydney for the start of the roadshow. There was a daily flow of telex messages between London, Tokyo and Melbourne and my 'Bible', a folder containing all the tour details, was swelling by the minute. Passport data, airline schedules, hotel reservations, limousine information, bodyguard and security details, and individual band members' specific drink and food requirements were recorded in the folder. Several cases of Dom Perignon 1961 vintage champagne had to be shipped from France as the champagne from that vintage was unavailable down under. Even the road crew's request for Brie cheeses had to be met.

The tour was scheduled to kick off with an outdoor gig in Auckland, New Zealand. In early January, the planning took a turn for the worst when the Japanese portion of the tour was abruptly cancelled. A disgruntled rival promoter in Tokyo leaked to the press an account of Keith Richards's alleged drug issues. To avoid the inevitable political backlash, the legendary Mr. Udo, the official Japanese promoter, pulled the plug. The tour was still to go ahead but was reduced to seven shows in Australia, one in New Zealand, and a possible gig in Hong Kong.

I flew out of Heathrow on a bitterly cold February morning, accompanying Mick Jagger's P.A. Pan American Airways handled flight arrangements, and the journey was arduous despite travelling First Class. Flight PA 001 was nothing more than a round-the-world flying bus service with stops along the way in Frankfurt, Istanbul, Beirut, Tehran, New Delhi, Karachi, Bangkok and Hong Kong, where we deplaned for a connection to Sydney via Denpasar in Indonesia. Each time we took off, another local plate of food was thrust under our chins, but at least the drinks continued to flow freely. The more intoxicated the P.A. and I became, the more we got out of hand, and somewhere over Cambodia, we made a ham-fisted attempt to join the 'mile-high club.' An unscheduled nine-hour stopover in Hong Kong broke the journey. A local record company executive, taking time to act as a tour guide, entertained us at the Peak Cafe, where we ate lunch. Dinner? Or was it breakfast?

Nearly thirty hours after leaving London, I staggered through immigration at Sydney's Kingsford Smith airport and out into a searing and humid 121 degrees Fahrenheit. Even in an air-conditioned limousine, my clothes were soaked when I checked into the Hyatt Kingsgate Hotel. Over the following three days, the band members drifted into town. Not unnaturally, Mick Jagger was confronted at the airport by members of the press who quizzed him about his wife Bianca's absence.

"Well, you don't take your missus to the office, do you?" barked an irritated Jagger.

The leading entourage members were registered in hotels under pseudonyms for security reasons. Names would change in each city visited. In theory, this all sounded good, but the reality was that rock and rollers paid little or no attention to such details, so by the third stop, no one had any idea who he was supposed to be. Maintaining a sporting theme, we went from footballers to cyclists and cricketers, at which point we remained until the tour ended.

Several 'specialists' were included in the tour party. Keith Richards had his guitar tuner, and his sole responsibility was tuning his guitars on stage before a performance. A baggage handler moved the luggage from the airport to the hotel to airport. His secondary responsibility was ensuring Keith's sound system was set up in his hotel room before the guitarist's arrival. A tour doctor was on hand to provide any necessary pharmaceutical requirements. Marshall Chess, head of the legendary Chicago-based Chess Records, was working on the finer details of a planned Stones documentary.

The band flew from Sydney for the first show in Auckland, New Zealand, to be held at the Western Springs Motor Speedway. In late summer, all the tour venues were outdoors in the Southern Hemisphere. The sporting locations included three tennis arenas, a horse racecourse, and a cricket ground.

News of the Japanese leg's cancellation had filtered down to the press in Australia, and certain conservative elements were looking for an incident to reinforce their opposition to the tour. No one was more vociferous than Bjelke Petersen, the arch-right-wing governor of Queensland. This cattle farmer enforced some of the country's most draconian drug laws and had already voiced his opposition to the Rolling Stones' visit to Brisbane.

I flew to the city to liaise with local Queensland officials before the touring party's arrival from Auckland. An ageing Lockheed Super Constellation prop plane had been employed to fly the sound and stage equipment from the mainland of the United States via Honolulu, Hawaii, to New Zealand. Brisbane was to be the first port of entry into Australia where a thorough customs inspection would be anticipated. I spent the afternoon with officials who assured me that a routine inspection would be a formality. However, when I reached the airport that evening, there was a small army of fidgeting customs agents nervously awaiting the arrival of the Lockheed carrying the freight. The aircraft landed just after 9 pm and, reminiscent of a tense hijack situation, was immediately surrounded by armed customs officials.

A leathery-faced, weather-beaten elderly pilot, a World War 11 veteran, emerged from the cockpit accompanied by his co-pilot, who was unconventionally dressed in sandals,shorts, an open-topped floral Hawaiian shirt and with his head adorned in a denim fly-fishing hat adorned with a pink Hibiscus blossom. He seemed discombobulated and was having difficulty staying on his feet. I spotted a customs agent grimacing at the sight of the ailing airman, and I sensed immediately that proceedings would not now be a formality. Over the next three hours, the officials systematically and methodically took apart the plane's cargo.

Australia enforces strict controls on importing overseas live or organic produce to prevent the contamination of its agricultural industry from external factors such as disease or pest infestation. So much so that passengers are routinely sprayed with insecticide upon arrival in the country before being permitted to set foot on Australian soil. Did they think we were transporting pineapples from Hawaii?

After what seemed like an eternity, the leading customs representative approached me, carrying a sealed jam jar containing what appeared to be a cigarette butt. It had been found wedged behind a speaker cabinet and was being taken away for a thorough forensic examination. Even if it turned out, as suspected, to be a roach from a marijuana joint, I would be unlikely to link it to the Stones as the equipment on board was regularly leased by other touring bands, and this 'dangerous cargo' could have been laid undetected for months. The official assured me that the issue was of little or no importance. I thanked him for his understanding and gifted him a pair of tickets for the upcoming Brisbane show.

The following morning, I awoke to read the headline news plastered all over the front page of the local Brisbane daily:

"DRUGS HAUL SEIZED FROM ROLLING STONES AIRCRAFT."

By the time the band's plane arrived in Queensland, the matter had been downgraded, and the authorities had gone out of their way to emphasise that the Stones were not personally implicated in the incident. The Brisbane show sold out within an hour of the box office opening, and it was reassuring to know that state officials had become aware of the potential problems a show cancellation would cause. An unseasonable tropical downpour forced the show to be postponed for twenty-four hours. By the following day, the weather had failed to improve, but taking their lives in their hands and risking electrocution, the band took to the stage to the delight of a drenched audience. The stay in Brisbane passed without further incident, although by the time everyone reached Melbourne, several of the road crew had developed symptoms of a common sexually transmitted disease. Fortunately, our tour doctor was on duty to provide the necessary treatment.

The 1969 tragic murder in California of a fan by a member of the 'Hells Angels' motorbike gang at the Stones Altamont concert had, in the eyes of many, demonised the band. And their music. Rumours abounded that the group had been performing the song, 'Sympathy for the Devil' at the time the fatal stabbing occurred. Whenever a scuffle or a riot broke out at a Stones concert, there was always the band and their satanic music to blame.

It was a sultry evening in Adelaide, with temperatures still in the upper 80s Fahrenheit. Inside, the stadium was packed, and outside, several thousand ticketless and disappointed fans had gathered in the hope that they still might hear the show from beyond the fenced enclosure. The authorities and police decided their presence was a breach of public order, and several dozen baton-wielding officers moved on the crowd. Water cannon was used to disperse the crowd, and police officers weighed in on unsuspecting youths. A hail of glass from broken bottles was landing beyond the fence, and I watched as a girl fell into the crowd from the broken branch of a tree. I tried in vain to get closer to the incident, but my arms were cut by glass shards raining down from beyond the fence. The band, oblivious to the ongoing scenario, were halfway through their set as victims of the police assault were stretchered into the stadium car park.

When not on stage, Mick Jagger, the ultimate professional, kept very much to himself. He skilfully handled the numerous press conferences with panache and would only leave the confines of a hotel to dine in the best restaurants that Australia had to offer. The bass player, Bill Wyman, and his wife, Ingrid, treated the tour as a working holiday. Each day and following breakfast, the couple, armed with guidebooks and a movie camera, would head out to visit the local tourist attractions. The drummer, Charlie Watts, kept very much to himself and became preoccupied with his family's situation, as they had been exiled to reside in France for tax reasons. I always thought that the guitarist Keith Richards never knew which country he was in, let alone which city. An endless supply to his hotel room of Jack Daniels whiskey and Cuervo Gold tequila, where his stereo system blasted incessantly, ensured that the revelling continued unabated.

I had spent the entire tour travelling with a suitcase full of tour party members' passports and international airline tickets. All that remained was to return the documentation to their respective owners and see everyone off on the flights out of the country. Bearing that in 1973, there were no mobile phones and no internet and any itinerary changes invariably involved trips to and from the airline office.

The trouble with rock and rollers is they would constantly change their travel plans, so it was not unusable for me to make numerous journeys daily back and forth to update flight tickets. Eventually, with the exception of one, all the group's leading members departed for their various destinations. The stereo blasted Stevie Wonder's 'Superstition' as I arrived outside Keith Richards' room. It was amazing that despite looking the worst for wear, the guitarist looked ready to leave. I bundled him into a limousine and headed to Sydney airport. I decided it was expeditious to handle Keith's check-in personally. Now was not the time for him to deal with awkward questions at the counter. Mission accomplished, I handed Keith his passport, ticket and boarding pass and pointed him toward the immigration counter. There was an uncomfortable pause whilst he stood silently staring at the floor. It seemed like an eternity before he turned and shuffled off toward the awaiting immigration official. The counter was less than 25 yards away, but barely halfway there, the guitarist turned around and doodled back towards me. I glanced over Keith's shoulder at an immigration official whose curiosity had been aroused.

Slowly, Keith proceeded to empty his jeans pockets, handing me a clear plastic bag of what appeared to be a stash of marijuana, a small zip-lock bag containing a white powder and five tablets of what was referred to as 'Orange Sunshine' LSD. He must have possessed some inner early-warning system that intuitively reminded him to dispose of any incriminating contraband. He turned and headed off, leaving me standing in the middle of Sydney airport with an assortment of illegal drugs. Before the paranoia completely overwhelmed me, I headed off to the nearest restroom, where I locked myself in a cubicle and flushed the weed and powder down the toilet. I removed a jar of aspirin from my briefcase, poured the contents down the toilet, and dropped the 'Sunshine' into the empty jar, replacing it with the briefcase before departing from the airport and returning to the hotel.

With work now over, I decided to rest and relax in Melbourne before returning to the UK. On my earlier swing through the city, I struck up a friendship with a local radio DJ, Mike Mussina, who offered to show me around. Shortly after midnight, after finishing his stint at the radio station, Mike showed up at the Southern Cross Hotel, where I was staying. Together, we smoked some Thai weed and continuously ordered room service to satisfy our ever-increasing appetites.

By four in the morning, the dope stash had dwindled dramatically, but neither of us wanted the occasion to draw to a close. I still remember the debacle of the night trip at the Roundhouse four years earlier before finally deciding to try Keith's 'sunshine' acid. We dropped the LSD and headed out of the city to the well-known country beauty spot, Dandenong Ranges National Park. Before setting off in the car, Mike had wisely decided to split his acid hit in two, estimating that the drug should begin to take effect around the time we reached the outskirts of the park. Mike's choice of Dandenong was twofold. Not only was this remarkable nature reserve a feeding ground for koalas, birds, and other indigenous wildlife, but it was also the habitat of the elusive 'Blue Meanie' magic mushroom, indigenous to Victoria and other Asian regions.

Encouraged by the enthusiasm of my Art School tutor, Will Clark, on the subject of magic mushrooms, I had enjoyed earlier experiences of psilocybin. Still, I had never heard of the 'Blue Meanie.' I couldn't imagine any respected mycologist naming a species after characters from the Beatles movie, 'Yellow Submarine.' Had Lennon and McCartney come across the mushroom on an earlier visit to Australia?

Dawn was beginning to break as we descended into the dense primaeval woodland. An overpowering stench of rotting and decaying plant life wafted upward from the forest floor, or was that the oncoming LSD beginning to grip the senses? I heard a rustling sound above a eucalyptus tree and spotted a mother koala and her cub breakfasting on the tree's foliage. A squawk from a lyrebird echoed through the forest canopy. All that was missing from this classic antipodean setting was a kangaroo.

Like an excited archaeologist ahead of me, Mike bent down on all fours, painstakingly scraping away dead foliage from the trunk of a tree. Several were nestling in the shade. Bell-capped green-blue mushrooms measuring about three inches in height. Within a few minutes, we collected about a dozen or so specimens. The heat of the early morning sun was beginning to penetrate the forest, and steam rose from the ground.

We headed back to the car and drove West to the coastal town of Brighton, where Mike and his mother resided. Considering our mind state, it is fortuitous that we arrived safely without incident. We spent the remaining morning hours beachcombing and, shortly after midday, decided to try out the mushrooms. Since picking them, the meanies had turned bright cobalt blue. We spread them on rounds of toast and washed them down our throats with a colour-complimentary glass of fresh orange juice.

NO-FAULT OF SAN ANDREAS

I was awakened by the airline captain's announcement that the aircraft would arrive at Honolulu International Airport shortly. I have always prided myself on how 'incapacitated' I sometimes found myself; I never suffered from short-term memory loss.

However, on this occasion and to this day, I have no recall of events following the ingestion of the 'Blue Meanies'. How had I returned to the hotel, travelled to the airport and made it onto the flight bound for San Francisco? To date, it has been my only 'lost weekend.' A beaming Polynesian maiden tossed an orchid lei over my head and around my neck as I stumbled through immigration, then reboarding the flight onward to California. I arrived in SF, checking in to a downtown hotel where I availed myself of the comfort of an American shower. I never fully understood that, at that time, showers in the States were so much more efficient than in the UK. Perhaps the demise of the British Empire was simply due to bad plumbing.

Refreshed, I took a cab to the Jefferson Airplane mansion at 2400 Fulton Street overlooking Golden Gate Park, where I was invited to visit. The impressive residence, with its Victorian facade and entrance, stood apart from other houses in the neighbourhood. I was greeted at the doorway by a young female brunette who, without any formal introduction, passed me a joint. In keeping with Californian dope-smoking etiquette, I took two tokes and passed the joint back. She smiled, turned, and hustled off into the building's dark, labyrinthine interior without saying a word. People were lounging around, engulfed in a marijuana haze, and music was blaring out from the upper floor. I bumped into an unknown individual who, sensing I was lost, offered me a joint. It became apparent that most people present were working on and for Timothy Leary's defence committee.

On September the 12th. 1970, the former Harvard psychology professor and self-proclaimed LSD guru, Dr. Timothy Leary, escaped from minimum security prison in San Luis Obispo, Southern California, where he had been serving a sentence for marijuana possession. From a safe house in the San Francisco Bay Area, he had headed East. Disguised and travelling under the alias of William McNellis, Tim was reunited with his wife, Rosemary. Together, they flew to Algeria by way of Paris, France, where they were to meet up with the radical Black Panther leader Eldridge Cleaver, who was living in self-imposed exile in Algiers. The Learys hoped Cleaver's influence with the Algerian authorities would facilitate a path towards being granted early political asylum. Still, the halcyon days of the 1960s were now distant memories for both Leary and Cleaver. The two now differed on fundamental ideological issues, irrevocably damaging their relationship.

Assisted by members of the notorious Brotherhood of Love, the one-time biker/surfing syndicate, the fugitives escaped their precarious situation and moved on to Switzerland. On his arrival, Tim was jailed while the Swiss authorities considered his case. The intervention of the mysterious Micheal Hanchard ensured that the Learys, without status or documentation, remained in the country for the next eighteen months. Hanchard's benevolence was to cost Leary half the advance on his book chronicling the prison breakout. His Swiss exile afforded him to meet for the first time Dr Albert Hofmann, the father of LSD.

They greeted one another at a cafe in Lausanne, where the excellent doctor proceeded to enunciate his belief that LSD was:

"An aid to meditation aimed at the mystical experience of a deeper comprehensive reality."

The instability and uncertainty of the Learys' future lead to marital tensions. When Rosemary confessed to an affair with an old acquaintance, their seven-year marriage ended abruptly, with the Swiss authorities rejecting his asylum application. Tim's morale was at its lowest ebb. Out of the blue stepped an English socialite, Joanna Harcourt-Smith. They dropped together 'windowpane' acid and instantly became inseparable. Intending on heading east to Ceylon, now Sri Lanka, the two inexplicably travelled to Kabul in Afghanistan. The city at the time was crawling with United States narcotics agents investigating the 'Brotherhood of Love' dope ring; Leary was spotted and, within four days, was on a flight to Los Angeles.

Joanna had taken up residence in San Francisco and was busy co-ordinating the funds for the escape-trial defence team, with the case due to begin in a few days. That evening, the quintessential West Coast psychedelic rock band, the Grateful Dead, was due to play San Francisco's Winterland ballroom, with profits from the gig going towards Leary's defence costs. The band's music, a fusion of rock and country, was never really my forte, but an invitation was extended to attend the show.

Rick Griffin was one of a select group of Bay area artists whose graphics and poster designs epitomised the counterculture movement of 60s San Francisco. His work included album cover designs and logo work for the Grateful Dead, which had a cult following throughout the United States. With the seat of my pants anchored to the pillion of Rick's Harley Davidson, we set off from the Jefferson mansion on a nerve-wracking high-speed drive to his studio. Sadly, his passion for motorbikes was to culminate in his premature death in a road accident twenty years later. His portfolio and prolific output were impressive, but an A4 sheet of paper decorated with a 'Dead' motif particularly intrigued me. My hunch was that it was a design for rock and roll wallpaper, but I was amazed to hear I was staring at a prototype sheet of LSD 'blotter!'

Until the early 1970s, illicit LSD had been marketed in three distinct formats. The liquid could be absorbed into the system by mixing with a drink or adding a droplet or two to an edible food substance such as a sugar cube. A measured concentrate of LSD liquid could be bonded with gelatine and cast into hard, translucent sheets, and the third form was pressed into pills. By utilising absorbent paper, such as a blotter, as a carrying agent. Up to a thousand doses of the drug could be impregnated into an A4 sheet. The sheets could be decorated with coloured decals, allowing artists to produce a new art form. One that could stimulate the visual cortex in many ways. This chance discovery was an entirely new outlet for my artistic endeavours.

At the entrance to the Winterland Ballroom, people were giving away tabs of acid like candy for a baby. I tried in vain to pay for a few hits, but the supplier refused to make any payment. The Grateful Dead played for over five hours to a jubilant, ecstatic crowd of tripped-out 'Deadheads.' The music was hypnotic and seamless, incorporating lengthy improvisational instrumental passages. The performance bore little resemblance to their recordings. They were a live band whose music, with the help of a willing and devoted audience, would reach a higher plane. The band's long, drawn-out passages of improvisation complimented the flowing, swirling imagery of the LSD trip.

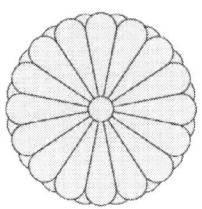

MUM'S THE WORD

Ishiro 'Itchy' Yukuda seemed to be London's only Japanese hippie resident. He was a master of networking; whenever there was a music industry event, he would attend. His name always appeared inextricably on VIP guest lists, but nobody had any idea how he made his living. We had first met a few months earlier at the 'Speakeasy' nightclub in Central London and exchanged telephone numbers.

I had been back in London for a couple of months when Itchy phoned to discuss a matter of mutual interest' so I invited him to the house for lunch. Linguistic differences apart, holding a conversation with Itchy would tax one's patience at the best of times. Drugs in Japan were strictly taboo, so since his arrival in the UK, Itchy had discovered the pleasures of hashish and spent most of the time in a blissful state of euphoria. Pensive and precise when attempting to verbalise his thoughts, his almost permanent stoned condition led him periodically to lose the plot halfway through a sentence. The final outcome of our extended lunch was a meeting with a Japanese businessman, Hideo Mimura.

In the wake of the sudden and unexpected cancellation of the Stones' tour of Japan, Mimura and his travel company proposed bringing a jumbo jet full of disappointed Japanese fans to attend the band's Autumn concerts in London and Paris. The only apparent unavailable and missing piece was tickets for the two shows, which appeared to have sold out months in advance. With my connections to the band, Mimura hoped I could resolve the concert ticket issue.

To establish his credibility, Mimura insisted that I fly to Tokyo to meet his partner and the project sponsors. Two days later, with Itchy in tow, I was on a flight to Japan. We were met at Tokyo International Airport by a white-gloved chauffeur for the journey to the Hilton hotel where I was to stay. On the drive into the city, we unexpectedly turned off the freeway at the Yokohama exit and pulled up outside what appeared to be a traditional Japanese villa shortly after.

We were greeted by four smiling, skimpy-clad women. Taking me by the hand, I was ushered by two of the women into a side room where, slowly and methodically, they began to undress me. Once fully naked, I was led towards a marbled jacuzzi. It was an ideal form of therapeutic treatment after an arduous transcontinental flight and all this before reaching my final destination, the hotel. The women's lack of English and my non-existent Japanese seemed immaterial. One in particular seemed fascinated by my body hair.

We were met in the hotel lobby by Mimura's business partner 'Akiosan.' After another perfunctory bowing session and before checking in at reception, we headed for the cocktail lounge. A bottle of Chivas Regal Scotch was brought to our table, and a travel company portfolio was presented. I declined the whisky offer, which appeared to disconcert the two partners. Had I offended them, or did they think I was aggrieved? I imagine they found it incomprehensible that an Englishman would decline a scotch. Their apology, though unnecessary, was quite touching. The only thing on my mind now was to get to my room and sleep. We adjourned, arranging to meet in the lobby the following morning.

That first night in Tokyo, there were two unforeseen episodes. I had barely reached bed when there was a knock at the door. It was the least attractive of the two bathhouse women, and she didn't appear to be on hand for an impromptu body hair inspection. Utilising improvised sign language and a dozen or so 'Sayonaras,' I managed without causing offence to persuade her to leave. My head barely touched the pillow before falling into a deep sleep.

I awoke feeling groggy and sore in my head. I glanced around and saw I was lying on the floor. I heard pattering feet and frightened voices coming from outside in the corridor. I slipped into a pair of boxer shorts, and as I opened the door to the room, the building shook, and I was thrown to the floor. Half-dressed bewildered hotel guests were streaming from their rooms into the corridor. The shuddering eased and came to a halt. An eerie silence descended. The city had just been struck by an earthquake measuring 6.8 on the Richter scale. This was my first encounter with such a force of mother nature, but it was not the last, as smaller temblors were commonplace during my later years in California. The damage to Tokyo's infrastructure had been superficial, but many of the city's dwellers had succumbed to the disaster.

Over the next day, and still not having fully recovered from the shock of the previous night's incident, I was bundled from one meeting to the next. I met and was introduced to a stream of advertising and television executives who did not fully explain what they had to do with the proposed visit of Japanese Stones fans to Europe. It transpired that in Japan it was essential to recruit sponsorship before marketing the project. This involved approaches to leading advertising agencies; additionally, a television documentary had been suggested. Once final decisions had been reached, we would reconvene in a few days. In the meantime, we were bound for Kyoto aboard the *'Shinkansen'* bullet train for a little R&R.

The ancient and former imperial capital was a perfect contrast to the bustling metropolis of Tokyo. With a newly purchased Nikon camera, I set out to visit the numerous Buddhist and Shinto temples dotted throughout Kyoto. It was a national public holiday, and I mingled with parties of inquisitive schoolchildren on the grounds of the Silver Pavilion, a two-tiered pagoda built on an island in a small lake. I left Itchy and Mimura at the hotel and set off alone. As the only Westerner present that day, it's quite disconcerting when everyone around you stares at you as if you were an alien from a distant planet. Having joined my two friends at a pre-arranged rendezvous, it was such a beautiful day that I decided it would be an ideal time and place to 'drop' some acid. I removed from my wallet one of the tiny squares of blotter I had acquired at the San Francisco Grateful Dead show and washed it down with a shot of Sake. Mimura was totally perplexed. He had just seen me swallow a small square of paper! There was an exchange between them, but then my efforts to succinctly explain the concept of set and setting to the guys proved onerous. Okay, so we were in a stunningly beautiful location, but what was their mindset? Nervously, they both agreed to take that first step into the realm of psychedelia. We headed over to the *Moss garden* where I roamed barefoot. The LSD had kicked in but Mimura kept insisting that he felt no noticeable effect. Somehow, we became separated, but strangely, I had no difficulty understanding myself. I clearly hadn't mastered Japanese, and most of the people I spoke with didn't speak English. Were we collectively speaking some hitherto unknown language?

Reunited back at the hotel, Mimura was enthused over his early adventures as a samurai warrior heroically slaying some sort of mythical beast whilst Itchy, obviously now totally westernised, had spent the afternoon on his hotel bed listening to Pink Floyd through his Walkman's headphones.

Following the all-too-brief recreational but thought-provoking break in Kyoto, we took the train back to Tokyo to draw up and finalise the details of the Stones concert package tour. After what was apparently a high-powered business lunch in the Chinzanso gardens, there were smiles, handshakes, and innumerable bowing, and it seemed the tour had been given the green light.

The LSD revelation had set Itchy's mind in a spin in more ways than one. He had already researched that a hit of acid in drug-starved Japan would command a price of $50.00. He was eager to set up a supply line should a source become available. I had a couple of possibilities through connections in San Francisco, so we arranged to travel home to the UK via the West Coast.

At 'The Saloon', a seedy but atmospheric blues bar on Grant Avenue in the bohemian district of North Beach, we met up with Rick Griffin, where we were introduced to his surfing buddy nicknamed 'The Babe.' From the bar, we were driven to the Mission district, stopping in the car park of a fast-food restaurant aptly named the 'Doggy Diner' from the roof of which gazed a giant grinning polystyrene spaniel. Babe introduced us to a supplier who outlined his proposition. A substantial amount of crystal was available, but the purchaser would be responsible for converting the product into tablets or blotter. Itchy seemed satisfied with the arrangement, and he and the supplier agreed to reconvene when the time was right to move forward with a buy.

David Parker, my regular squash partner in England, was in his final year of a doctorate in pharmacology at London University. Personally, he had had no experience with LSD. Still, as a chemistry graduate, he was familiar with the drug's synthesis and had meticulously described to me, in obtuse 'scientific' English, the chemical procedures that would be utilised. Depending on the number of purification processes employed, the final product, a powdered crystal, would range in colour from a bright sparkling white through light grey to pale amber. Soluble in various liquids, it could easily be recrystallized, particularly if the solvent used was fast drying, such as Methanol. An alcohol-based solution was also a practical method for transferring the LSD to blotter paper. Pill pressing the drug was more complicated than simply soaking and impregnating a sheet of absorbent paper.

Over the years, resourceful drug cartels and dealers have employed ingenious methods to transport their products safely to market. Southeast Asian heroin smugglers even control their private armies to escort caravans of pack animals through hostile territory en route to landing strips or coastal staging posts. A network of aircraft or ships moves the illicit cargo onto their final destinations in Western Europe or the United States. The annual profits from the trade of illegal drugs have made the trade the World's third most valuable industry.

As law enforcement agencies worldwide discover the smuggler's modus operandi, more ingenious concealment methods must be utilised. With a bottle of duty-free vodka, the LSD smuggler can pass undetected through most customs controls, transporting 400,000 doses with an estimated street value in Japan of up to $2,000,000. Barely an ounce and a half in weight, this relatively small amount can be dissolved in a litre bottle of spirit alcohol such as vodka. Rendered invisible to the naked eye, it's the simplest and safest method of transporting the product from source to distributor. Once beyond border controls, it's a straightforward procedure to transfer the impregnated liquid to blotter paper.

Beside the hotel's swimming pool, over freshly made margaritas, Itchy and I discussed the details of the dealer's offer. We agreed that my only involvement would be primarily supervising the design of the blotter, the final printing and perforation of which would be carried out in Japan. I settled on a simple but appropriate chrysanthemum design, a symbol traditionally reserved for Japan's Imperial family. Alone, I flew back to London.

Once back home in the UK, I carried out some preliminary research into inks and paper grades. The final print run was planned for two sets of colours on white and another colour background. The chrysanthemum design had been photographed and was ready to be transposed to a lithographic plate in Japan. The funds for the buy had been wired in separate smaller batches to avoid the United States Treasury currency regulations.

The first afternoon back in Japan was spent trying to explain the complexities of the print job to a confused local printer. I left his print shop with a selection of paper samples, planning to test them later in the evening. I headed to the Roppongi district of Tokyo for a reunion with Mimura, who was relieved to hear one hundred fifty tickets had been reserved for the London and Paris shows. At the end of the evening, we celebrated with numerous carafes of warm sake. I was bundled into a cab and whisked back to the Imperial Hotel. It was too late to test the paper samples, so I awoke with a blinding hangover the next morning.

Over the years, I have used the services of many lithographers and printers to produce finished blotter paper, but none have surpassed the quality fashioned for that first commission. The finished sheets were beautifully wrapped in washi paper, a product manufactured from local fibre, which was made in a traditional manner and tied with gold thread. Over the next few hours, I laboured painstakingly dipping 100,000 hits of LSD. All that remained was to put the final product to the euphemistic 'acid test.'

Itchy's suggestion that we spend the time tripping in the oriental gardens surrounding the thirteenth-century bronze Buddha of Kamakura was inspired. The forty-four-foot-high statue, a benign smile exuding from its face, stares at the viewer from a meditative lotus position like an Oriental 'Jolly Green Giant.' Normally, it's impossible not to be impressed by this imposing figure, but under the influence of LSD, I felt like Swift's Gulliver arriving in Brobdingnag. I threw up a discussion with the statue, much to the bewilderment of the Japanese onlookers. I was convinced I was having some sort of deep metaphysical conversation with a godlike figure. I guess the acid worked.

That afternoon in Kamakura was the last time I saw or ever spoke again to Itchy.

KRITI CALL

I spent most of 1973 away from home in London. During my absence and probably partly out of need of companionship, my wife Eva's sister had joined her from Sweden. By the time I had returned from Japan in November, another of Eva's girlfriends had moved into the house, and I felt like a stranger in my own home. Increasingly, we lived separate lives, and as our relationship waned, we drifted further apart. Professionally, my life turned in an entirely different direction as I began to work at a school teaching art and photography.

I struck up a friendship with Julie, the head of the geography department, and we soon began an affair. Her partner had sensed her infidelity, and her domestic predicament grew precarious. In Early March 1975, fearing for her safety and my marriage effectively over, the two of us, anticipating turmoil and avoiding the freezing weather, eloped to Greece. We had no concrete plans for the future. All we knew was we were in love and finally together.

On a mild sunny spring morning, we landed at Athens International Airport. For initial accommodation, Cat Stevens' father, the wily Mr. Adams, had recommended a quiet family-run pension in the seaside suburb of Vouliagmeni. The following week, the old man arrived to spend the Greek Easter with the Athenian half of his family. Julie and I decided to travel to the island of Crete in search of a quiet, secluded and romantic location where we could idly spend the summer months. So, to arrange passage and be accompanied by Stevens' father, we set off from the hotel for the bus to Athens.

At the stop stood an English couple: she was in a faded Laura Ashley floral dress, and he was in Khaki knee-length shorts, grey woolly socks and open-toed sandals. The pale-skinned duo from Manchester had just begun their holiday. Cat Stevens and his father had always had a turbulent relationship, but the old man was tremendously proud of his youngest son's achievements. He always carried a pocketful of black and white portraits of Steven wherever he went.

"This is my son, Cat Stevens," he remarked, thrusting the picture under the woman's nose.

The couple's expressions spoke volumes. 'Was this a street peddler trying to palm off his wares?' They turned their backs and scuttled off into the distance. That evening, we sailed from the port of Piraeus aboard an overnight ferry bound for Crete, docking finally early the following morning, just before sunrise.

Sfakia, the Southwestern province of Crete, is an unforgiving, rugged and mountainous region. In 1941, relentlessly pursued by a German invasion force, the tattered remnants of a British Army corps scrambled down the cliffs to the beaches, where they were plucked to safety by a small flotilla of Royal Navy warships. In Dunkirk's tradition, another glorious retreat was added to the annals of British military history. The successful extraction of the survivors was due in no small part to a heroic role performed by the native Sfakians, who harried and killed the advancing German paratroopers who were attempting to thwart the escape.

After the successful extraction, the Germans decided to exact revenge on the Sfakians. Still, they came up against a tough and resilient guerilla movement, who, despite their numerical disadvantage, were never entirely subdued by the occupying forces. The Sfakian's reputation as a feared resolute people has endured, although internecine disputes and vendettas have continued to plague the region's politics. To this day, fearful mainland Greeks and even Cretans from the Eastern part of the island still refuse to travel to Sfakia. Had the guidebook alerted us to these facts, perhaps we might have been dissuaded from setting foot in the village of Loutro, but then we would have cheated ourselves of a once-in-a-lifetime experience. Nestling in the lee of a crescent-shaped bay and at the base of a 1500-foot peak, the village is only directly accessible by sea. In 1975, there was no tourist boat service direct to Loutro, so Julie and I bartered with a fisherman to ferry us the five kilometres from the port of Chora Sfakion.

Yanni, minus his right hand, missing in action whilst dynamiting for fish, steered his boat alongside the jetty, and we stepped down from the bow onto a pebbled beach. Facing the dock were two whitewashed single-storey buildings and a Venetian-styled facade of what loosely could be described as a pension, owned and operated by the elderly village battleaxe, Marika. Overlooking the picturesque harbour and bay was only one room to stay. The room had two single beds and cleaned and pressed sheets, but for £1 per night, this was luxury. We unpacked and freshened up under a drizzle of brown water from a rudimentary shower and returned downstairs for a bite.

Outside on the terrace, we sat at one of only two tables, anticipating a waitperson would arrive shortly with menus. Darkness had fallen, and the village was pitch black save for the light from a kerosene hurricane lamp dangling above our heads from the pine tree branch. A resinous smell lingered in the air. Ten minutes passed, and nobody had appeared at our table, so I poked my head around the front door of the pension. My sudden presence must have disturbed the black-clothed figure lying inside on a bench. An elderly, hunched lady struggled to her feet and snarled. In my broken tourist guidebook Greek, I politely enquired if it wasn't too late to eat.

"Mono omeletta!" Marika replied tersely. Just omelette?

Within minutes, we were served plain omelettes cooked on a one-ring propane burner and swimming in spicy green olive oil. We soaked up the oil with stale bread and washed it down with warm beer. It may seem slightly banal to say that a good omelette is down to the eggs used, but the eggs of Marika's simple dish that first night in Loutro made all the difference.

The following morning, we were shaken abruptly from our slumber by the sound of gunfire. Curiosity aroused, we hastily threw on some clothes and scrambled down onto the terrace. Outside the front door of the adjacent building sat the fisherman and two other Cretans. Using the stump of his missing hand as a rest, the fisherman struggled to aim a rifle toward a rusty tin can perched precariously on a bollard at the end of the jetty. He discharged several rounds, landing harmlessly beyond the intended target and into the sea. The three friends were in good spirits, and the spirit was in them. They sat there joking and laughing between liberal swigs of Raki, the local firewater distilled from grape musk. Yannis' two friends looked more like freedom fighters than shepherds from a neighbouring mountain village. Each wore a fully equipped bandoleer strapped across his chest. Tethered to a tree nearby was a nervous-looking mangy sheep, its rear hooves bound together.

Leaving the revelers to their amusement, we ambled 100 metres along the beach towards the village centre. Altogether, no more than fifteen houses were laid out haphazardly in a three-tiered arc back towards the base of the mountain. A scattering of mulberry, almond and pomegranate provided minimal shade for the buildings, whilst at the foot of the village on the fringe of the beach stood a solitary mature palm tree. It was by far the tallest structure in the town and dominated the landscape. In the shade of the palm fronds, a young man was struggling to descale the hull with a crude, rusted tool of a beached and upturned fishing dinghy. Further along, an overweight woman waded up to her waist into the calm waters of the bay and was busy scrubbing and washing clothing. There was nobody else around. The village was almost deserted. The only sound is the occasional gunshot from Yanni and his friends.

Most of the two-story houses were shuttered and closed. The shabby, ill-kept buildings looked like they had remained uninhabited for some time. An ageing woman dressed head to toe in black, a head scarf tied tightly under her chin, was drawing water from a rudimentary well. We greeted her with a customary 'Kalimera' as we stumbled along the rocky path that bordered her garden. Julie seized the moment to enquire about the availability of a house to rent, and the old lady gestured for us to join her indoors. We were offered green almonds and raki, which, just after ten in the morning, is a little too soon to imbibe. The daughter Joanna appeared, and with her passable English, we were able to explain our wish to rent a house for several months. We agreed to return later when two properties would be available to view. On our way back down, the young man we had spotted earlier working on his boat introduced us to another villager, Stella, who also seemed to be in the local property rental business. We viewed a two-storey house at the back of the village and, within minutes, handed over the monthly rental of $10.00.

Having secured accommodation, we returned to Marika's pension to gather our belongings. We arrived just in time to witness a shepherd, now sufficiently inebriated, slitting the tethered sheep's throat. It writhed and screamed, but it was all over in an instant. We watched in morbid curiosity as the Cretan herder skinned, bled the animal, extracted the entrails and swiftly removed the coat and outer skin. After that, this spectacle was repeated whenever a shepherd arrived to trade meat for fish.

In addition to the native population of 18, Loutro's population swelled by five with the addition of ourselves, Rosemary, a German medical student who took Greek lessons from the handsome village doctor and a couple from France. Yves, a youthful, radical left-wing journalist and writer, would be travelling to Argentina at the end of the summer whilst his partner, Beatrice, bourgeois, bleached blond hair and twenty years Yves senior, would be returning to her former employment in an exclusive cosmetic salon located on the fashionable Rue Faubourg St. Honore. Their views and opinions were from the opposite end of the political spectrum, but not unlike Julie and me, they also had discovered the charm, tranquility and idyllism of Loutro.

The five of us became friends, and once a week, each would take turns accompanying Yianni to the next village, Chora Sfakion, to purchase groceries, as all provisions in Loutro would only arrive by sea.

Later that summer, Nico, a retired sea captain and Loutro resident began operating a daily tourist ferry service between Chora Sfakion and the famous gorge of Agia Roumeli, located 20 kilometres west of Loutro. In the evening, after disembarking the last of his passengers, he would sail back to Loutro laden with supplies for the villagers.

Even if Yanni could discover the motivation to cast his nets or dynamite, fish were rare in this part of the Mediterranean. On one occasion, I was fortunate to barter for a spiny lobster from a Libyan Sponge diver. In vain, I spent hours each day, to no avail, hunting for seafood and armed with a spear gun. However, around each full moon, sea urchins were in abundance, offering a delicate sweet roe from within their spiked outer casing.

All our meals were cooked on a terrace over an open fire made from olive branches and twigs. Our diet was simple but classic Mediterranean—aubergines, courgettes, tomatoes, onions, cucumbers, pulses, bread, cheese and village wine. The rental house's interior was a skeletal shell, but we only spent time indoors sleeping at night or during the afternoon siesta. From our bed with the shutters open, we were blessed on a moonlit night with a panoramic view of the majestic palm tree and the Libyan Sea beyond.

Our first week in Loutro coincided with a seasonal storm. It was cool, overcast, and rained incessantly for three days, but the locals assured us that once the storm had passed, we could expect continuous sunshine until the end of the year. The rain finally stopped, the clouds dissipated, and the skies cleared. Setting off on a narrow dirt path leading from the village to explore the surrounding area, our eyes were filled with an awe-inspiring array of brightly coloured wildflowers. The inclement weather had brought forth a host of rare orchids and unusual spring flowers, which felt at odds with the barren rocky terrain. Within a week, spring had come and gone, and only the scattered wild mountain marjoram was to endure the heat to bake the arid landscape in the coming months. Weather forecasts headed our list of information deemed surplus to requirements. We enjoyed no television, radio or newspapers. Wars could have been declared, fought, lost or won, and we would have remained none the wiser. The only certainty was that each new sunrise would yield another day of relentless sunshine and heat. Once or twice that summer, a mighty intercontinental wind blew in from the Libyan desert 150 miles away, depositing a film of red dust over everything.

Loutro was well and truly off the beaten track. During our six months in residence, only a handful of foreign tourists strayed into the village, most of whom were disorientated hikers who had stumbled on the village by chance. The exception was the renowned explorer Jacques Cousteau. Late one afternoon, the village was returning to life after the daily siesta when the roar of a helicopter's engine shattered the serenity. Fitted below the plane's fuselage were two hot-dog-shaped bright yellow floats, each inscribed in black letters with the word 'Calypso'. The circling aircraft quickly surveyed the harbour and bay, then banked and flew off to the West. Any connection with the famous French explorer hadn't yet registered in my mind, but thirty minutes later, the intrepid oceanographer's survey ship 'Calypso' dropped anchor in the harbour. Swimming ashore, the bronzed strapping sailors who emerged from the sea expected a hero's welcome, but their expectations were shattered when they were ignored completely. They soon returned to the mothership, having suffered almost as severely as Captain James Cook's unfortunate arrival in Hawaii. On other occasions, the village's tranquillity was disrupted, but external factors did not bring them about.

Often, after a busy week ferrying tourist back and forth, the crew of the Nickolaos would let their hair down. All night drinking sessions involving themselves and anyone who could stay the course would take place inside an innocuous small, blue-painted wooden shack—owned by the village elder Stavros with just a rectangular wooden table, four chairs and standing room for ten. The interior walls were bare, save for one, plastered with postcards from various eras worldwide. The building served no practical purposes except as a venue for the occasional drinking session. One of the alarming facts about these events was that the majority of participants carried handguns. As more and more raki was consumed, one by one, victims would tumble to the ground, eliciting a volley of gunfire from those remaining standing. I soon discovered that the purpose of the postcards was not purely decorative but a practical and straightforward way to cover the bullet holes.

These events were the only excitement to disturb the tranquillity of such an idyllic, stunningly beautiful and romantic location. It would be difficult to imagine anywhere more perfect to begin my rapidly developing love affair with Julie. On reflection, the stay in Crete was one of the most memorable periods of my life. The pressures of the music industry and the stress of teaching had been left far behind, and I was now totally at ease with the pace of life.

Once a week, the distant blast from the mountainside from a cow horn signalled the imminent arrival of the postman, his round taking him across the mountains and down to the coast on a thirty-mile journey. In late July, I received an unexpected letter from The Babe, the LSD connection in San Francisco. I had no idea how he had tracked me down to this remote spot on a Greek island, but the request was for a meeting in Amsterdam in late September.

Julie and I decided to spend two weeks island hopping, and together with Beatrice, we travelled north to the island's capital, Heraklion. By ferry, we sailed first to Mykonos, then to Ios and Paros before returning to Loutro. We were surprised to discover that Yves had left the village in our absence, but the story of his sudden departure left us in disbelief.

Whilst ferrying from Agia Roumeli, Yves had become agitated over the ship's captain's flirtatious behaviour with a young French girl.

The Frenchman had had a fling with the same girl earlier in the year. For whatever reason, Yves had chosen to intervene on the girl's behalf, and a heated argument ensued. Later that evening, the crew returned to Loutro with Yves in tow, frog-marched him at gunpoint to the ruins of a Venetian fort and forced him to dig his own grave. He was severely beaten by his captors, kicked into the open trench and warned that if he remained in the village the following morning, he would be taken up to the fort, shot and his body buried where he now lay. Our blissful summer had ended on a sour note, and within a week, we left the village heading for Amsterdam. On Christmas day, a lightning bolt struck the imposing village palm tree, bringing it crashing to the ground. Loutro was to change forever.

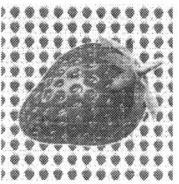

STRAWBERRY FIELDS

The Hotel Torenzicht in the heart of Amsterdam's 'Red Light' district was to be our home for the next four weeks. The narrow canal-side corner building consisted of eleven quaint single rooms laid out over three upper storeys. On the ground floor, a tiny breakfast room backed onto a cozy, intimate bar where, at night, the hotel's owners 'Tigre' and Hubert, held court. Every so often, local peep show or brothel owners would stop in to pay their respects to the two, who were considered the neighbourhood's most respected but feared 'entrepreneurs.'

It didn't take an Einstein to figure out that the hospitality business was not exactly Tigre and Hubert's primary source of income. On the surface, the two exuded charm and generosity, but I always got the impression that incurring their displeasure, the likelihood of being found floating face-down in a canal was a distinct possibility. The hotel's clientele, an assortment of transient escort girls and out-of-town dope dealers, were all on first-name terms with the two Dutch dons. I often witnessed Hubert placing or removing suspicious brown paper packages behind the cigarette machine, and not long after, someone else would arrive to deposit or collect them. The hotel was a constant den of intrigue, and Julie and I were viewed as an incongruity that did not quite fit the mould. Our new residence in Amsterdam was in sharp contrast to the idyllic and rustic time spent on Crete.

There were ongoing delays with the Babe, who was still in California. In the interimwe enjoyed Autumn in Amsterdam and soon decided to stay over the winter months. Following a successful interview at the Amsterdam International School, Julie was hired to teach English and American history during the fall semester. A multinational institution, the fee-paying school fulfilled the educational requirements of the children of the city's growing international business community. Julie's knowledge of American history was less than basic, but like any experienced teacher, she was more than capable of bringing her knowledge up to the required standard in no time.

I arrived at the pre-arranged rendezvous, the bar of the Krasnapolsky Hotel, where I met up with The Babe and an associate in time for 'happy hour.' Gone were his bleached locks and casual clothing, replaced by a neatly parted and trimmed shock of black hair, a sober business suit, a starched white shirt and a necktie. He looked like your average American corporate executive over the Atlantic on company business. The associate, who was travelling as an academic, hailed from Boston and spoke with a heavy Massachusetts accent. The kind of drawl that turns 'park' into 'paahk' and 'dark' into 'daahk.'

Like many Americans, The Babe's knowledge of World geography ended abruptly at Staten Island. In his mind, Europe was just like any state of the Union, where you could just hop on and off an airplane and be anywhere on the continent in a few hours. The idea that I had to journey by fisherman's ketch, bus, ferry boat, subway, taxi, airplane and finally a train just to get from Crete to Amsterdam was completely beyond his comprehension. It reminded me of the German girl, Rosemary, in Loutro receiving a letter from a friend in Berlin requesting that she be met at Loutro's 'Hauptbahnhof', the main railway station!

I was nevertheless curious why our meeting had been set for Amsterdam. It couldn't have been a mutual appreciation of Dutch 17th-century painting or a love of tulips! On my recommendation, we headed to a well-known local Indonesian restaurant. The Babe's bewilderment suggested he would have difficulty locating Indonesia on a map, let alone getting his head around a traditional Balinese 'rijsttafel.' His business was straightforward. He had several hundred thousand doses of acid already in Amsterdam and needed blotter in two weeks.

The 'assistant' had spent his formative years in New England, raised in a strict secular Judaic environment in which his father served as cantor to the local synagogue. Eager to extricate himself from the clutches of his conservative background, he enrolled in the early 1960s in an organic chemistry course at UC Berkeley in California. Not unlike many of his contemporaries at that time, he soon became embroiled in the counterculture movement, dropped out before his finals and moved into a commune in Bodega Bay, just north of San Francisco. On learning that their son had hooked up with a Mormon girl from Salt Lake City, his family back in Massachusetts disowned him.

He had first met the Babe at a Grateful Dead concert, who, on learning of the New Englander's chemistry background, soon put him to work. With the offer of a comfortable and profitable lifestyle, the two became partners in an LSD enterprise. The Babe had mentioned to him my previous brush with rock and roll royalty and, like others before him, was eager to know all the inside details of life on the road. I outlined the farcical daily list of sports personality pseudonyms involving the Stones, and he immediately pointed out his cover name and the Babes were former baseball stars. Ted Williams had been a Boston Red Sox icon, whilst 'Babe' was the all-time Bronx bomber, Babe Ruth. I was immediately christened Willie Mays, former San Francisco slugger.

Over the next hour, my ears began to ache as 'Ted' went into the smallest detail concerning the Beatles and the *'Sergeant Pepper'* album. Every conceivable conspiracy theory and crackpot story was laid bare. Top of his list was the 'discovery' of Paul McCartney's death, which becomes apparent when the album is played backwards! Surely there are better ways to pass the time? For a so-called expert in the subject, he seemed surprised and upset to discover that his favourite Beatles tune, 'Strawberry Fields', was not a brand of LSD but a Salvation Army shelter in Liverpool. I felt a sense of guilt at having shattered his allusion and resolved to make it up to him in some way.

I was new to Amsterdam, so there were numerous logistical problems to overcome. To minimize any risk, I would have to ring separate outlets for printing and perforation. I decided to enlist the help of Tigre from the hotel, who, within 24 hours, had provided discreet options for handling the work. Once completed, I took a sample sheet to Ted, whose face lit up when he opened and removed a field of strawberries from the manila envelope.

The greatest of plans, sometimes for one reason or another, have to be shelved and an alternative devised. The LSD's client was in Australia and, nervous about having a blotter shipped to him, sought an alternative. He now wanted unperforated paper the surface of which had to appear marbled. Each sheet was to be inserted into the inside and back cover of a consignment of books. I tinted the liquid LSD with a brown pigment, refrained from stirring, fully blending and, with a swirling movement, tried to recreate a marbling effect. I first practised on a couple of sheets that just stained slightly brown in water. I was as surprised as anybody that the finished product looked authentic.

Just before the onset of Winter, Julie and I moved out of the 'Red Light' district to the suburb of Osdorp. Our modern two-bedroom apartment had a direct view of Amsterdam beyond the Sloterplas Lake. In addition to her school teaching Julie had taken on private English tuition, two of whom were the children of the president of the *Banco do Brasil*. In his early thirties, the Brazilian moved rapidly up the corporate ladder. His role in the company was that of a troubleshooter who was sent to supervise and open a new branch of the bank each time. Overseeing and ensuring a smooth transition before moving on to another branch opening. His platinum blonde-haired wife came from a Brazilian aristocratic backgroundand her family lived in a castle on their own private island north of Rio de Janeiro. I found their Neo-Nazi salutes and the clicking of heels with fellow Brazilians a disturbing greeting, but regardless of their political stance, he and his wife were both kind and generous to

Julie, and we had an open invitation to stay with them should we ever visit Brazil.

My former squash partner, David Parker, had finally received his doctorate and had recently taken up a post as a research chemist at a UK-based pharmaceutical company. Although well-paid he found the work mundane and unfulfilling. He was newly married but his life lacked excitement. In his phone call, It seemed that things were improving. He sounded upbeat and ebullient. He needed my advice on a delicate matter which he felt could only be discussed face-to-face. I collected David from the airport in my newly-purchased second-hand former police VW beetle. His news presented several intriguing possibilities. An ex-fellow student had introduced him to a mysterious Henry Todd who, having wined and dined David, outlined a proposal. With apparent access to a substantial quantity of ergotamine tartrate, the LSD precursor, he was looking for a skilled chemist to synthesize the drug. Henry had not revealed any further details, but an offer of a considerable amount of money was on the table. From the bedroom, I took the original artist's proof of the 'Strawberry Fields' blotter and having brought David up to date on the distribution method, we sat up late to discuss the feasibility of the project. By the time we went to bed, David had spent his advance three times over. on the trappings of consumerism. He was already envisaging his stately home and the red Ferrari parked in the driveway. He and his Bostonian counterpart, Ted Williams, share many similar traits. Both came from sheltered upbringings, had remarkable analytical minds, and were qualified chemists, but they were both socially inept. I left any final decision to David, but ultimately, I felt he would eventually bottle out of the venture. The matter and any discussion involving myself never came to fruition. A few years later, Henry Todd was to be arrested and implicated in *'Operation Julie'*, the largest LSD bust in Europe to date.

FREE WAY

The Winter of 1975 was the severest Holland had suffered in many years. A freezing cold Arctic front had moved in from the Northeast, the icy wind cutting into the body like a laser through steel. For the first time in 20 years, all the canals froze, and on weekends, the Dutch took to their skates, turning the waterways into a scene from a Brueghel landscape. On Christmas day Julie held an open house for a disparate group of expats. Present at the customary seasonal feast were two Americans, a Scot, a Moroccan, a French woman, a New Zealand couple and a native Bangalorean who arrived bundled up like an Eskimo.

In Holland, especially amongst the older generation, there still existed a strong undercurrent of resentment towards immigrants. This was even more pronounced towards citizens of the two former colonies of Suriname and Indonesia. This brand of racism was clearly open to see in South Africa where the Dutch settlers, Afrikaners, were instrumental in imposing apartheid (A Dutch word) on the indigenous population. This was one of few blemishes on the nation's character: a people of great charm, acerbic wit and genuine hospitality. A multilingual society whose communicative skills made them renowned international traders.

The Winter may have been bitterly cold, and tourism reduced to a trickle, but with the approaching springtime and milder weather, Amsterdam began to swell with tourists again. The canal boats were back in service, and the sound of the organ grinder echoed from the *Kalverstraat*.

For Julie and I, it would soon be time to point the car towards the Southeast and head off back to Greece and our final destination, the island of Crete. On arriving back in Chora Sfakion, we were surprised to see there was now a daily ferry sailing to Loutro. On board were a dozen or so backpackers. Our secret paradise was no more! The discoloured and weathered trunk of the palm tree, severed from its roots, lay rotting on the beach. Marika's pension sported a new freshlypainted sign in English and German and lighting and refrigeration were now provided by way of a generator. Adjacent to the pension, the one-handed Yianni had opened a brand-new fish restaurant, every available house was already rented, and there were now sixty tourists living in the village. We stayed a couple of weeks, long enough to work on a decent suntan and soon after, we departed on our return journey to Amsterdam.

We were back barely a week in the city, and even though it was summer, the thought of another Winter in Holland was less appealing. We considered taking up the Brazilian banker's offer of a trip to Rio but he and his family would be abroad until the beginning of the new year. In the interim, I suggested we take a leisurely drive starting on the east coast of the United States and heading cross country to California. Available at that time and throughout the States, was a driveaway scheme where, for merely the cost of fuel, travellers could deliver cars on behalf of the owners from one city to another. One's driving license and passport details would have to be registered with the FBI, but ample time was given to make the delivery. We hung around the New York office for a day, hoping to get a coast-to-coast single drive, but we had to settle for a car to Chicago from where we could pick up another drive going west. It was early October, but snow had already fallen in the Northeast, and we were still dressed in summer clothing. From Chicago and driving a brand-new Chevrolet van scheduled for customization in Houston, Texas, we meandered south, hugging the eastern bank of the Mississippi River. From Cairo, Illinois, mile after mile, cotton plantations were laid out for as far as the eye could see. That evening, we pulled into the historic town of Vicksburg, Mississippi, the site of a famous Civil War siege. According to our guidebook the 'Old Southern tea rooms' was one of the South's finest down-home country cooking establishments.

An overweight 'momma' who looked like she had stepped out of the film, 'Gone with the Wind,' dressed as she was in a red and white check apron and matching knotted kerchief, precariously balanced atop her head. Served up was an enormous, deep-fried catfish, accompanied by humongous portions of grits and cornbread, neither of which, to this day, I find particularly appetizing. The meal's consolation was the mint juleps. Bourbon, bruised mint leaves, cracked ice, but unfortunately distastefully decorated with flags of the Confederacy. Sunday morning, whilst Julie remained under the bed covers nursing a hangover, I wandered down to the motel's bar for a 'kill or cure' bloody Mary. I was the first customer of the day. A giant TV screen dominating the lounge was showing an American football game. I settled into a comfortable leatherette banquette to take in the bizarre spectacle of two armour-clad teams hell-bent on pummelling one another into submission. Naming the game 'football' seemed a misnomer as in fifteen minutes of viewing I never saw anyone kick the ball. A well-built muscular African American with an oversized neck sat down beside me to watch the game. He was an avid fan of the game and triumphantly raised his fist in support of the team in black shirts and tight-fitting gold Lurex pants every time they advanced with the ball. Seeking some brief clarification of the tactics and plays of the game, I leant towards him and apologized in advance for my ignorance, It turned out that the stranger was a college football star from Jackson, the state capital of Mississippi and coincidentally had recently attended a try-out for the professional team in black and gold I was viewing on-screen.

A group of scowling 'rednecks' uniformly dressed in faded overalls and molded cream plastic cowboy hats had gathered at the bar. The footballer grew uneasy and, to my surprise, got up and, without so much as a goodbye, left the bar. Call me naive but I remained oblivious to what had happened. I crossed to the bar to order another bloody Mary and the group of farmhands parted like the Red Sea. On hearing my accent, the tension that I sensed receded.

This may have been 1976, but there was no good reason for a 'white boy' to be seen talking with a 'nigger.' unless he was a real outsider.

Even with a two-day break in Vicksburg, we arrived at Houston ahead of schedule. On the drive into the city, we pulled into the vast complex of the Astrodome and convention centre. The day before, the sports arena had been packed with adoring fans, but on this Monday afternoon, only the ground crew could be seen on duty. Across the car park stood a scaled-down version of the Astrodome, the convention centre. Outside fluttered a row of red, white and blue bunting above a sign that read:

'Annual National Convention of Morticians and Funeral Directors.'

We tagged along with the crowd streaming into the building. We were greeted by a smiling usher who provided 'guest' badges and we roamed around the cavernous interior. Displayed on a vast revolving plinth were several examples of ornate coffins and sarcophagi. Silver with gold handles, polished ebony inlaid with ermine, mahogany, maple, brass, granite and marble. Every imaginable material had been utilized to ease one's passage into the next world. There was even an elaborate reproduction of a pharaonic Egyptian barge complete with decorative faux hieroglyphs. I had to admit that some of the financial terms on offer seemed quite reasonable. $5.00 a month over the next fifty years seemed more than affordable! I was confronted by a salesman who was more than aggrieved when I revealed my desire to be cremated after death. His pained expression suggested that I had just driven a stake through his heart. Anyway, there were plenty of options for him to lie down and recover.

Jan Van Wouters had emigrated from Holland ten years previous. Having worked his way up the ladder of the hospitality industry and following on from an acrimonious divorce, he had relocated from Houston to Arizona and was managing a resort hotel in the affluent city of Scottsdale, a short drive from the state capital of Phoenix. A cherry red Chevrolet four-wheel drive 'Jimmy Blazer' was all that he had salvaged from the divorce settlement, yet he could hardly believe his eyes as I brought the vehicle to a halt in the driveway of the hotel. I neglected to mention that had we not survived a hair-raising accident, skidding in a snow blizzard on a deserted mountain pass in New Mexico, then our and the vehicle's twisted remains would be lying at the bottom of a gorge remaining hidden from discovery until the Spring thaw. His joy turned to amazement when I pulled from a hold-all a bottle of rare Dutch Jenever that I had nursed all the way from Amsterdam.

Unable to find a ride further west, we took a flight to Los Angeles, hired a car and took a leisurely drive north along the Pacific Coast Highway. Gazing out over the Pacific, we finally were on the other side of the globe. The winding scenic drive took us past the folly of Hearst's Castle, Henry Miller's hunting ground of Big Sur, and our journey ending in the town of Palo Alto. This sleepy little town, lying forty miles south of San Francisco, owes its existence to one of America's most prestigious institutions of higher learning. Stanford University.

I had met Jonathan two years earlier under difficult and painful circumstances whilst we were both patients at Hampstead General Hospital in North London, requiring similar surgeries to an identical and embarrassing part of the anatomy that left us recuperating face down on our stomachs. A friendship and mutual empathy developed over our two weeks of convalescence together. Finally able to sit in a seat again, Jonathan, on his release from hospital, had returned home to California. We remained in touch, although my telephone call from Monterey came as a bit of a surprise as I hadn't previously briefed him of my travelling to California. Since his return from the UK, Jonathan had moved home to Palo Alto, dabbled in Zen Buddhism and mysticism, toyed with gardening as a profession and smoked copious quantities of marijuana, which undoubtedly accounted for his general lack of motivation. Nevertheless, he was most hospitable and offered the use of his battered VW beetle should we need to visit San Francisco. He welcomed us both with open arms. I telephoned the Babe in San

Francisco, notifying him of my arrival, but caught him at the wrong time as his beloved Yankees baseball had just lost the World Series to Cincinnati. For the Babe baseball preceded everything else in his life. The phone call was curt, and I was asked to call when I was next in the city.

The day Julie and I drove into San Francisco there was a reason to feel optimistic. A relatively unknown peanut farmer from Georgia, Jimmy Carter, had swept aside the bumbling Republican President Gerald Ford and the Democrats were back in the White House. I had talked up the city with such enthusiasm that Julie's first visit could have been anticlimactic. To my relief and surprise, she fell instantly in love with San Francisco, and within an hour, we were searching for an apartment to rent. Etched into my memory was my first meeting with the Babe atop Twin Peaks, gazing down on the panoramic sprawl of the city and the sun-drenched district of Noe Valley. By lunchtime, we had found and rented a quaint coach house set back at the rear of a grand Victorian Mansion.

Entry into the United States was on a three-month tourist visa that could, with an appropriate reason, be extended to six. Without the necessary 'resident alien' documentation and the illusive *'Green Card'* we were barred from working. We were running low on funds, but in a typical Micawberesque moment, I believed I could rely on the Babe for a commission. My heart sank on hearing that my potential source had left town for an undisclosed destination and for an indeterminate period of time. Any form of legitimate employment would require a social security number and a California driving license.

We strolled into the social security office of the quiet suburban town of Woodside, ten miles from Palo Alto. Our choice of this branch was deliberate as we believed we would be less likely to arouse suspicion in a white upper-middle-class area rather than the multi-ethnic community of San Francisco. Our pitch was that we were freelance journalists spending an extended working vacation whilst researching local issues. We said that we had been advised that after three months our British or International driving licenses would no longer be valid. We would now require a valid California Driving License and obtaining one would necessitate a social security number. We filled in all the paperwork with our newly-rented apartment as our place of residence, and two weeks later, our social security cards arrived by mail. To this day, I still don't know if the number is required to obtain a California driving license, but it seemed a good enough reason at that time.

The next stop was the Department of Motor Vehicles, commonly abbreviated to the DMV. After completing a multiple-choice written questionnaire, a photo session, and a supervised drive around the car park, we were issued Californian licenses. Although we lacked 'green cards,' our social security numbers meant we could now legitimately pay income tax, and as far as the Internal Revenue Service (IRS) was concerned, that was all that mattered.

By melding her culinary skills with her teaching prowess, Julie obtained a position as a cooking demonstrator with a well-known and exclusive San Francisco cookware store. The store, which caters primarily to the wealthy, does a roaring trade in truffle slicers, asparagus peelers, and hand-carved bone caviar spoons. This place is so chic that even its copperware pans are silver-plated.

One of the fringe benefits of touring with famous bands and musicians was the accessibility of fine wine and champagne. I discovered that once you are exposed to great French Bordeaux or Burgundy wines, you are less likely to drink a box of wine or a Portuguese rose from the supermarket. I think, in general, fine wine is a boy thing. You turn to it with age, like cars, once you have abandoned those childhood hobbies.

It didn't take too long to convince a soon-to-open restaurant that my expert oenological knowledge was needed to construct an award-winning wine list. Californian wines were at last receiving international recognition and it wasn't long before local vintners lined up at the door of the restaurant. There is a certain social acceptance of becoming light-headed at a tasting; besides, if you can't stomach what you are drinking, then spitting out a glass's contents is an integral part of a taster's duties. Having ploughed two million dollars into the venture, most of which was absorbed by decor and furnishing, the investors discovered all too late that they had overlooked the minor detail of a chef. The *St James Restaurant* was to close its doors for the final time two months later.

Our first Christmas Day in California was spent in 70-degree sunshine. We breakfasted outdoors in the shade of a blossoming bougainvillea. We left home early in the afternoon for a movie matinee at the Castro Theater. The building had retained much of its Art Deco interior from the 1930s, and pre-show entertainment was provided by an organist playing the theatre's original *Wurlitzer*. In true Gothic style, the musician and his instrument were raised to the stage through a trap door and a cloud of smoke. We returned home two hours later, having watched Katherine Hepburn and Spencer Tracy rekindle their off-screen affection in 'Keeper of the Flame', The title of which would resonate for me later in life.

A contact from the St. James' restaurant debacle presented me with the opportunity to organize and supervise a small catering event in Palm Springs, Southern California. For the grand opening of the latest edition of fine ladies' hairdressing salons, I was flown down to the desert resort city. The event was attended by a scary collection of Republican dowagers, the majority of whom appeared to have suffered under a plastic surgeon's scalpel. Apart from receiving an overly- generous fee for my services, the only other notable episode was an invitation to meet the deposed bumbler Gerald Ford and his dear wife Betty, who were the guests of honour at the gala event.

Respectful in the presence of American 'royalty' the crowd parted as the former President and First lady entered the building. There was no redcarpet entrance, and far from appearing regal, the bumbler was dressed in a hideous pair of lime green polyester pants and a pink polo shirt, having just arrived from the golf course. Poor Betty dressed in a pastel summer dress, looked frail, gaunt and glass-eyed. She seemed not to quite know where she was and needed her husband's assistance to negotiate the two marble steps leading to the salon's entrance. Given the bumbler's poor track record with staircases the ex-president stumbled and tripped in public on more than one prior occasion), I thought Betty showed great courage in relying on Gerald. Looking like she was suffering from the rigours of substance abuse, I found it ironic that in her name she should later sponsor the famous drug and alcohol rehabilitation clinic!

Bizarrely, I was asked to give an interview to a local newspaper in which I gave the recipes for the buffet dishes served at the opening. I guess nothing of real interest ever happens in Palm Springs. I flew back to the sanity of San Francisco.

It was officially the first day of Spring. Not that one really notices the coming or passing of Winter on the California coast. When the telephone rang, the Babe's voice was the last I had expected to hear. It had been almost five months since his Houdini disappearing act, and I had no idea how he had tracked me down. In the interim he had been idling on the beach in Mexico's Yucatan, in the town of Tulum. He had returned home just in time for baseball's spring training programme. It appeared that his whole life's order of events was centred around the game of baseball. He seemed genuinely pleased that I had settled in San Francisco. We met up at a taqueria in the city's Hispanic Mission district.

This meeting turned out to be a seminal moment in our professional relationship. For the first time, I was to understand the fundamentals of a select band of individuals who had dedicated themselves to maintaining, if somewhat limited, an underground supply of LSD. A collection of individuals that coincidentally the Babe had christened 'The Keepers of the Flame.' This small group, now living outside the law and keeping very much to themselves, did not fit the criminal mould. They never contemplated mass production of the drug, had no expressed interest in generating huge financial profits and operated as a cottage industry, unconcerned by external market forces. Production to distribution occurred only twice a year and, on each occasion, lasted less than a month. Once completed everything shuts down for another six months. For the past fifty-odd years, and unlike every other illegal drug, there has never been a continuous supply of LSD. Large-scale operations have come and gone, but there have been periods of drought, and the drug has, at times, become unfashionable. Over a ten-year period, the Babe had discreetly built up a small network of clients throughout the world, only ever adding to his 'portfolio' a hitherto untapped region. Ichiro ('Itchy') had only been successful in acquiring a consignment as there was no previous arrangement with Japan. Depending on how his beloved Yankees baseball team fared that season, the Babe would not be back in production before September at the earliest.

Julie had successfully established herself as a professional cooking teacher, now working freelance, giving classes and demonstrations throughout California, whilst I picked up some consultancy work in the catering industry. The more time passed, the more we fell under the spell of San Francisco. With the possible exception of New York, there is no other city in the United States that has such a cosmopolitan European feel. The city hosts opera and ballet companies, a symphony orchestra, repertory theatres, numerous art galleries and the largest cross-section of ethnic restaurants a gourmand could possibly wish for. The city's liberal-leaning meant that Chinese, Hispanic, Japanese, Russian, Irish, gay and lesbian communities co-existed harmoniously and collectively; the varied cultures and lifestyles enhanced the city's character. Even Palestinians contributed, operating corner stores and mini-markets. In all the years I have resided in San Francisco, I have never actually felt like I was living in real America.

To the north, across the Golden Gate Bridge, the pleasures of the wine-growing regions of Napa and Sonoma often beckoned. There was no better way to pass a summer afternoon than picnicking in the Sonoma foothills with a bottle of local wine. To the east, a leisurely drive through the Sierras retracing the route of the gold prospectors of 1849, southbound the Pacific Coast Highway (PCH), the alluring ruggedness of the Big Sur National Park. Once or twice, I accompanied Julie on business excursions to Los Angeles, but the novelty of Southern California would wear thin after a couple of days, and I would be desperate to return north. There is no love lost between San Franciscans and Los Angelinos. The acrimony that exists between the two cities is best illustrated by the late and renowned Bay Area newspaper columnist Herb Caen.

"Isn't it nice that people who prefer Los Angeles to San Francisco live there!"

However, that veneer of San Francisco refinement would be unpeeled for the visits of the Los Angeles Dodgers. The genuine dislike for the rival baseball team from La La Land was always prominently expressed on the mushrooming car bumper stickers that read:

"Fuck the Dodgers!"

Over the course of the summer, I worked on several blotter design options, and having narrowed the field down to three, I arranged to meet up with the Babe and his chemist, the uninspiring Ted Williams. I drove towards Telegraph Hill, onward and upward as it spiralled anti-clockwise, eventually coming to a halt in the car park of the 'Julius Castle' restaurant. A mock Crusader building complete with turrets and battlements.

Ted's former Mormon wife had long abandoned him and joined a Hare Krishna Ashram in Poona, India. Her absence was reflected in his lifestyle change. The apartment reeked of decaying food matter, the kitchen sink overflowed with unwashed crockery, and the bathroom washbasin and toilet were stained and discoloured. Ted's black and curly hair and ungroomed beard were tangled and matted. Dressed in a grubby olive-green T-shirt and military fatigue trousers, his appearance resembled a jungle freedom fighter. The Babe turned out to be a no-show, and feeling more than just uncomfortable in Ted's hovel, I tossed the designs on the table and made my excuses for a quick and early exit. Etched still in my mind was the wretched condition Ted had been reduced to.

Had I not been distracted then I might have noticed the dark mound lying ahead in the centre of the road sooner. A parked car's flashing hazard lights indicated that there was insufficient space to pass so I was left with no option but to come to a halt. I stepped out of the car and walked towards the obstruction. As I closed in on the mound, I noticed a trailing darkened liquid oozing forth and trickling downhill. The bullet's entry had left a clean hole in the young man's left temple. I could hear him hyperventilating. Moving closer I saw that the exit wound had blown away the right side of his head. Not knowing what to do, I looked around for help and spotted an ashen-faced elderly guy transfixed by the sight of the horror that had unfolded. On the ground, between his feet, I could make out the silhouette of a handgun. The victim's rapid breathing came to a halt and his body lay motionless. Not being able to help a dying man, my immediate overwhelming feeling was one of impotence and frustration. The street was deserted save for the despairing old man, a taxi driver. The lights of his vehicle flashed continuously. On informing him the young man had died, he broke down and sobbed uncontrollably. The police arrived at the scene, and after a brief interview, the taxi driver was handcuffed and taken into custody. When I reached home, I was unable to sleep and sat up and, with a deep personal sense of remorse, wept most of the night. The following day after the shooting incident, I received a call from the Babe, who said he loved the 'Burning torch' blotter design I had left at Ted's apartment. Any enthusiasm I had previously was tempered by the thought that the night before another flame had been needlessly extinguished.

Living in San Francisco, sometimes one imagines one is cocooned from the harsh realities of everyday life in real America, but tragic events involving guns will continue to haunt the nation until the Second Amendment of the Constitution is re-examined. Later I read in the local newspaper that the taxi driver was found guilty of involuntary manslaughter and jailed.

New Year's Eve, 1979, and partygoers and revellers were gearing up for the city's traditional Grateful Dead concert. The band's former renowned sound engineer, Owsley Stanley, had more than a passing interest in chemistry and had established himself as a producer of LSD of the highest quality. He and the Babe were close friends, and therefore, it didn't take a rocket scientist to figure out there was probably a business connection between the two of them at one time. However, on this occasion, Babe was awash with 'Windowpane' acid, the product of the chemists Nick Sands and Tim Scully. A meet had been set up close to the concert venue, but when the Babe arrived, he was arrested by undercover federal agents. He was caught with several thousand hits in his possession. For an international supplier whose transactions normally ran into hundreds of thousands this bust was a double-edged sword. Fortuitous that the amount in his possession was relatively small, his choice of client had been injudicious. Forty-eight hours laterhe was arraigned and bail was set at a million dollars.

On hearing of his partner's arrest, Ted went on the run and hid out in Half Moon Bay, thirty miles south of the city. Fearing his partner might reveal his identity, he began making frantic efforts to raise the deposit for a bail bond. His best shot was Babe's father but locating him was no easy matter. Now retired, he travelled extensively and, at that time of the year, could be anywhere from Costa Rica to Tahiti.

In the late 1950s, the father was a US government employee and was rumoured to have worked on the CIA's covert chemical warfare programme, MK-ULTRA. Under pressure from the US Congress, the research work was finally closed, and the old man took early retirement. An unconfirmed rumour was that he had had access to ergotamine tartrate, the precursor to produce LSD and from this source, Babe and Ted were receiving small amounts on an annual basis. Was it conceivable that indirectly, the CIA was partly responsible for the continuing supply of LSD?

Fortunately for Ted, there was no incriminating evidence at his Telegraph Hill apartment but returning to the residence was too risky. At least he had been smart enough to have made contingency plans in the event of a snafu. Stashed away in a safety deposit box were two passports: one fake, the other genuine, and $30,000 in cash. In addition, there were two plane tickets. Under the fake passport's name was an open round-trip ticket from San Jose to Puerto Vallarta in Mexico, and the second, in his real name, was an open one-way ticket from Mexico City to Madrid, Spain. The absence in his real passport of an entry visa into Mexico from the United States would not necessarily arouse suspicion as up until the 911 terrorist attacks, thousands of Americans would pass daily back and forth into Mexico using just a valid driving license as the only form of identification.

I agreed to collect the contents of the box, on his behalf, collected him from his motel and we drove a few miles up the road to San Mateo. At a shopping mall, Ted bought some luggage and a new summer wardrobe, and we drove back south to San Jose International Airport. Before his departure I handed Ted the address and phone number of a friend in Madrid whom I could rely on to take care of the soon-to-be-fugitive until the problem back in San Francisco was resolved. Dressed in a gaudy Hawaiian shirt and tinted glass he looked like an ugly American tourist.

Having faced drug conspiracy charges, Babe was sentenced to twenty-five years with the judge's recommendation that he remained incarcerated for a minimum 15-year stretch. My early LSD involvement had come to an unforeseen and abrupt end.

Six months later, after having trawled through the brothels of Barcelona, Ted returned to the United States. He hadn't exactly found a replacement for his ex-wife, but his sexual exploits had drained his resources physically as well as financially. He needed to get back to work sooner rather than later. The Babe's father was back in the Bay Area, having spent the winter south of the border. Out of contact, he had only recently heard of his son's arrest and imprisonment.

It wasn't long before Ted was required to synthesize a fresh batch of LSD. He was unquestionably a skilled chemist who was constantly striving to improve the quality of his work. Rightly, he had no knowledge or interest in where or how his product would be distributed, and it was now left to me to recover and repair the damaged line of communication with the European market and, specifically, the Amsterdam connection. Rather than having supplies of impregnated blotter run the risk of crossing transcontinental border controls, it was safer for the blotter to be produced at its final destination. Overseas clients were encouraged to print and perforate their own paper, and I was dispatched to provide the technical know-how. Some clients couldn't manufacture the paper themselves, so arrangements were made to ship unimpregnated blotter separate from the LSD liquid. The impregnator, or 'dipper' would collect the paper and the liquid from their separate destinations and then dip them in the host country. Deliveries to Amsterdam, Rome and Athens were completed first in Springtime and then once in the Autumn.

Ted's studious New England upbringing gave him a better grip on World geography than the Babe, but in 1982, when I discussed a possible trip to meet an Australian client in the New Hebrides, even he was unaware of the location of this archipelago. He assumed I was planning to journey to an isolated group of islands off the Scottish mainland. Did it seem reasonable that I should travel 7000 miles and the client 12000 to transact an LSD deal?

TROUBLE IN PARADISE

Ten years earlier, whilst working on the Rolling Stones tour of Australasia, I had received an enquiry from a company based in Port Vila, the capital of the then New Hebrides. More intriguing than the mundane contents of the correspondence was the fact that the company's telephone number was listed as a radiotelephone number via Paris, France. This antiquated system, invented in the 1920s, was primarily a means of voice communications between a shore or ship telephone via a marine operator. In some respects the system had been the antecedent of the modern mobile phone. Here was one of the last remaining countries without a direct international telephone connection.

The collective group of islands was known as the New Hebrides Condominium, as it was jointly governed and ruled both by the United Kingdom and France. It was a bizarre situation where there existed two legal systems, two separate civil services, two police forces and, of course, two official languages as well as numerous Melanesian dialects spoken by the indigenous population. Its only historical claims to fame were that the northern islands were used as a staging post by the allies in World War 11, and the writer James Michener, whilst based in the New Hebrides, wrote his first book, later to be turned into the musical, 'South Pacific.'

Almost two hundred years after the first Europeans had set foot in the islands, the indigenous population of Melanesians was finally about to achieve independence from their British and French colonial masters. In another ten days, the New Hebrides would become the Republic of Vanuatu. The Australian client, an inveterate mariner, was currently at sea aboard a 45-foot catamaran heading towards Port Vila. On his arrival, he intended to participate in the international regatta, one of the many festivities marking independence. At the conclusion of the race, a shipment of newly dipped blotter would be delivered to his boat, and once secured, the intrepid Aussie would set sail back to Queensland.

Julie and I jetted from California to Fiji a week ahead of the courier, Francois, and then onward to the New Hebrides. This allowed sufficient time to collect the blotter paper and be set to dip once the acid arrived. Following on from our stay in Fiji, we flew north to Port Vila on the island of Efate, touching down at a remote airstrip carved out of a vast grove of palm trees. A small primitive shingled hut with a thatched roof of woven palm fronds passed for the airport terminal and once we passed through the immigration formalities, we and the other disembarked passengers were shuttled through an open side door. Beyond, we found ourselves on the way back to our parked aircraft, where we each were required to collect our own luggage as no baggage-handling service was available. Heavily laden, we re-entered the terminal through the same doorway and were waived on through, foregoing any form of customs control.

My expression of disbelief soon turned to shock and bewilderment as, on exiting the building, I was confronted by a squad of heavily armed French paratroopers! Had we not spent the previous days in San Francisco focused solely on our travel plans, then we might have caught newspaper reports that an armed insurrection had broken out in the New Hebrides. Fearing that the transitional independence government would nationalize their holdings, a group of French colonial copra farmers on the northernmost island of the archipelago, Espiritu Santo, had fermented an armed rebellion intent on seceding from the remainder of the country. Financed and partly instigated by a shady businessman from Phoenix, Arizona, whose plan was to construct casinos and establish a tax-free zone.

Several violent skirmishes had broken out, and a dozen or so native Melanesians had died at the hands of the rebels. Determined to quash the uprising before the changeover of power a company of Royal Marines arrived from the United Kingdom to join their French paratrooper comrades who had flown in from the nearby French colony of New Caledonia. Martial law had been declared, and a dusk-to-dawn curfew imposed. Our anticipated tropical utopian setting had transformed into a war zone, and worse news was to follow. The Sheraton Hotel, our pre-arranged accommodation, had been commandeered by the military and was functioning as operational headquarters! With accommodation in Port Vila at a premium owing to the influx of dignitaries invited for the forthcoming independence celebrations, we settled into a traditional colonial bungalow. Tucked away on the outskirts of town, the house would provide some necessary seclusion and privacy.

The first task was to ensure that the blotter paper had arrived safely. The consignee was a New Zealander whose local harbour-side eatery served as a watering hole for the island's colonial residents. Every Friday, British and French expat civil servants, local politicians and administrators would gather at the restaurant, where affairs of state would be discussed and settled. With the sudden and unexpected attention of the world's media focused on these remote islands, the dining room was packed to the rafters. The sole remaining seats were at a table shared by two hacks from an Australian daily newspaper and a portly English doctor who hailed from Dorset. The affable gentleman had newly arrived, seconded from having spent the previous year in the even more remote British territory of The Pitcairn islands, where he had served the community of the descendants of Fletcher Christian and the 18th-century mutineers from *HMS Bounty*. Gorging themselves on the local delicacy of the steamed coconut crab, the journalists were doing their best to deplete the restaurant's wine cellar and were guzzling their third bottle of French white, Burgundy. Reports had come in on the wire service that the rebellion had been quashed and the situation was now fully under the control of the French and British military forces. I discovered that the two press gluttons had camped out in the shore-side restaurant for the entire campaign, syphoning off Reuters reports, editing the content and forwarding on to the UK as 'In-depth coverage.'

Like any journalist they were naturally inqusitive and eager to know what I was doing while visiting the distant and remote outpost of the waning British Empire. My cover story was that I was a philatelist awaiting the release of the first-day cover commemorative issues from the newly independent Republic of Vanuatu. Considering my involvement with decorative sheets of perforated paper the cover story dovetailed perfectly. Showing a distinct lack of interest in the world of postage stamps, the hack's conversation quickly changed to the up-and-coming exhibition cricket match due to be played the following day.

I hadn't yet met or been introduced to my New Zealand contact. Whilst the journalists droned on about the state of English cricket, out of the corner of my eye, I spotted a rugged individual perhaps in his late thirties. Attired in a sailor's bellbottoms, blue and white hooped T-shirt and white rubber flip flops, he looked like Hollywood's idea of a French 'matelot'; he was moving from table to table greeting the guests. Mr. McMillan, the much-admired proprietor of the restaurant, had not left a positive impression on the good doctor seated at our table. There were rumours that gun-running had been one of his dubious business activities and that he had fled New Zealand.

Although LSD's illegality is classified in the same schedule as heroin and cocaine, major cartels or crime syndicates have never controlled its manufacture or supply. Most of those involved had been introduced to LSD in the 1960s and maintained idealistic views on the drug. It would be naive to suggest that professional criminals were never involved to some extent along the chain of supply, but to the best of my knowledge, I had never known such individuals until my encounter with the swarthy New Zealander.

For the first time, I began to feel ill at ease. I was stuck on a Pacific Island swarming with commandos and paratroopers, and my only contact was an alleged international gun-runner and smuggler. Now was not the time to make my presence known to the burly Kiwi. I wrestled with the 'special of the day', the novel dish of 'fruit bat bourguignon,' and listened intently to the doctor's fascinating account of tribal medicine within the islands.

Having successfully drunk themselves into a near stupor, the hacks retired to the press office to create their latest in-depth report, whilst the doctor departed for the hospital in time to relieve his native colleague who had an urgent appointment with the local witch doctor for treatment of her menstrual cramps.

Having settled the bill, I dawdled over a brandy until all the remaining diners had departed. The dining room's walls were adorned with brown sepia photographs of the town of Port Vila dating back to the 1920s. It was a sobering thought that cannibalism was still, at that time, a common practice in the islands, a concept that seemed hardly surprising if the example of local cuisine I had just consumed was anything to go by! A restless waitress had posted herself directly in my line of sight and was going through the motions of a well-rehearsed routine, alternating between glaring at me and glancing at her watch. The owner arrived on the scene, and pre-empting his move, I offered my hand and a friendly wink.

According to McMillan, my client, who turned out to be his brother-in-law, was due to dock in the early hours of the following day. The courier, Francois's flight, was due to arrive at 6 pm the same day, and if everything went as planned, I could begin dipping that same evening. Needing a clear floor space approximately 40 feet long and 16 feet wide, McMillan offered the restaurant dining room which would remain closed throughout Sunday. I admired his sense of the theatrical, transforming the town's centre of intrigue into a temporary LSD gallery. The tables and chairs were stacked against the walls, leaving ample room to lay the sheets of impregnated blotter on the floor. The restaurant's three antique Victorian ceiling fans would hasten the drying process, and the entire endeavour would be complete by Sunday evening. Julie had waited up for me, unaware of my activities. I used the excuse for my late return as a few drinks with the locals.

As a child I collected British Empire stamps as a hobby and as my cover, I presented myself as a stamp dealer. After all, I was in the business of sheets of perforated squares not too dissimilar to postage stamps. Given the island's imminent independence, the occasion was ideal to acquire first-day covers from the local Poet Vila post office.

I spent most of Monday recovering from the exertions of the previous twenty-four hours and, accompanied by Julie, headed into town for dinner at a Czech restaurant. How incongruous a Bohemian plate of dumplings and wild boar felt in the middle of the Pacific but then nothing was normal in the New Hebrides. As we left the restaurant, an argument broke out in the street between an East Londoner and a French Gendarme over an apparent traffic infringement. Absurdly, the policeman had no jurisdiction over the Englishman, and a British 'bobby' had to be summoned to make the arrest. With dual educational, legal, judicial and health authorities functioning simultaneously in the country, it was a miracle that a permanent state of schizophrenia didn't afflict the inhabitants.On Independence Day morning, I headed to the post office, reinforcing my cover story by purchasing a stack of first-day commemorative covers. After lunch, Julie and I made our way to the cricket ground. There was a victorious march-pass by the visiting troops. Taking the Royal salute on behalf of Queen Elizabeth at the Republic of Vanuatu's inauguration ceremony and dressed in military uniform was the Duke of Gloucester. A huge barbecue had been arranged for later that day but the government of the fledgling democracy got off to an inauspicious start by imposing an alcohol ban on all non-whites. A few documents had been signed and hands were shaken but the status quo had not changed one iota. A twilight curfew was still in place for the non-whites, and only the high-spirited colonials were permitted to stay out and watch as that evening, Vanuatu's first annual budget went up in smoke on an elaborate firework display.

The following morning, whilst still in the throes of alcoholic poisoning, I struggled to focus on the armada of ocean-going yachts as they headed out from Port Vila's harbour and into the open sea. The 200,000 hits of LSD were on their way.

As our Air Nauru Boeing 737 arced southward, I stared back down at the islands of Vanuatu. What hopes and expectations did the islanders have for their futures? The immediate outlook was not promising, and teething troubles and difficulties lay ahead, but at least their destiny was now in their hands. Maybe they should open a casino or two?

In December 1981 my final undertaking of the year was a trip to South America to provide 'technical assistance' to the Babes' longest-standing client. In his late teens, Carlos Delgado had relocated from his native Uruguay to Buenos Aires, Argentina, to pursue a degree in economics. In the late 1960s and early 1970s, nowhere were the times more turbulent than in South America. Half the continent was under military dictatorships, propped up by hawkish anti-communists in Washington D.C., whilst radical left-wing politics had made dramatic inroads in the remaining countries. Soon after his arrival in Argentina, Carlos abandoned his Capitalist-inspired studies and joined a Marxist student fraternity.

When his life came under threat from the ruling military junta, he fled to Sao Paulo in Brazil, joining a network of leftist students operating in the state. Whilst there, he was introduced to the power of the hallucinogenic vine yage. The psychedelic experience was to have a profound effect on him, and his studies drifted away from politics and towards a meaningful study of psychoactive substances. Through a fellow student, he acquired his first LSD tab and, henceforth, never looked back. Over the next ten years, his former student network became the primary conduit for the drug in South America and the Babe his source of supply.

Having previously encouraged other clients to produce their own blotter, I was on my way to Peru to supervise the paper's printing and impregnation. The courier, Francois and I travelled separately but on the same flight, which had originated in San Francisco, stopping only once in Los Angeles on its journey south to Lima. In the charming coastal area of Miraflores I met up wiith Carlos at the beachside restaurant *Costa Verde*. The Uruguayan expressed his sympathy for the fate that had befallen the Babe, asking me to pass on his condolences to his absent friend. We moved on to the aptly named 'Sergeant Pepper's Bar', where I sampled the delights of Pisco sours. We joined a group of obstreperous Americans who invited us to the American Consul General's residence. The diplomat had been recalled to Washington, and his private secretary had the weekend off and the freedom of the house. I made an excuse and bid adieu, having been cornered for most of the night by a gibbering cocaine-fuelled embassy employee from Akron, Ohio. I never get over the verbal diarrhoea that always seems to spew forth from those high on cocaine.

Every major South American city seems to have its showcase neo-classical Grand Plaza, but once you venture beyond the facade, the stark contrast between rich and poor becomes all too apparent. Squalid shantytowns where the impoverished indigenous Indian communities struggle to survive. Lima was no exception, and in its poorest districts or barrios, those who could afford a semblance of footwear wore sandals crudely cut from car tyres. The stench of urine and excrement was overwhelmingly nauseous. I've witnessed poverty in India and Southeast Asia, where somehow people manage to maintain some dignity, but the utter feeling of despair etched in the faces of the barrio's inhabitants left me scarred.

I had provided Carlos with an Inca design and had gone over the impregnation process numerous times until I was satisfied it was indelibly stamped in his mind. The most popular and common soft drink in Peru is the appropriately named 'Inca Cola', unlike its universal cousin 'Coca Cola,' which is coloured lime green, so it seemed only right that the purple Inca image should be printed on an acid green background. The paper had to be ordered from outside the country and its arrival was not expected to be for another five days.

Iquitos in Northeastern Peru lies on the west bank of the Amazon and accordingly experiences a tropical rainforest climate. It rains most of the year; more often than not, it's a deluge. The weather was a sharp contrast to the beaches of Miraflores, where I had encamped on my arrival in Peru. A chance conversation with Jurgen, a German fellow traveller had led him and me north to the Amazon region, where we were to meet up with an entourage of Westerners with the sole purpose of participating in a shamanic ritual encounter of the 'sacred vine' Yage. More commonly known as Ayahuasca.

I had a fundamental understanding of the nature of the experience, having read William Burroughs and Allen Ginsberg's book *The Yage Letters*. However, like most things psychedelic, you never know what you get until you try. My previous peyote 'journeys' in Oaxaca, Mexico, meant I thought I was fully prepared for the inevitable 'purge', but having drunk the murky liquid, there was an immediate onset of imagery and the worst vomiting experience I can recall. The previous week, on the train journey from Cusco to the ruins of Machu Picchu, I had buried my thoughts in the writings of Inca mythology, specifically the writings of the supreme deity Viracocha. During my yage experience, Viracocha came to life in the shaman's body and soul. The image that forms the basis of my first NFTs is the face I envisioned forty years ago during that memorable Amazonian experience.

I returned 'cleansed' to Lima and just to be safe, oversaw the blotter impregnation. Later in the day, I spent relaxing on the beach, where I struck up a conversation with an English-speaking Peruvian woman who worked as an airline stewardess for Braniff Airlines, the very airline I and Francois would be taking on our return journey to the States. In passing she mentioned that that particular flight had a dubious reputation and was colloquially referred to as the '*Cocaine Express.*' Its final destination was San Francisco but its first port of entry into the United States was Los Angeles. Whilst disembarked passengers made their way through the immigration formalities, a team of customs agents would board the parked aircraft, carrying out a rigorous search for any contraband that may have been stashed before deplaning. Any drugs uncovered would be replaced in their hiding place, and returning passengers attempting to recover the goods would be taken into custody on arrival in San Francisco.

On my arrival at Lima airport, I found Francois anxiously pacing back and forth. He was perspiring profusely; his eyes were sunken into their sockets and his gaze was wild. He was nervous, edgy and looked like he hadn't slept in a week. His erratic behaviour was beginning to draw the unwanted attention of the airport's military security guards. I tried to ignore him, but he shadowed me wherever I went. He was to reveal that he was carrying a kilogram of pure cocaine but was getting cold feet and uncertain how to discreetly dispose of the drug.

Anyone in earshot could have overheard his remarks. The mere association could implicate me in a cocaine smuggling conspiracy. I had a nightmarish vision of imminent arrest with the possibility of a minimum fifteen-year and a day prison sentence. I turned around and fled towards immigration. After an uneasy flight during which I spotted Francois visit the toilet on numerous occasions, the aircraft touched down at LAX, Los Angeles International. At immigration, I was grilled over my visit to Peru and, using my philatelist cover story from the New Hebrides/Vanuatu, presented my business credentials as a bona fide stamp dealer. However, I was escorted to a side room, strip-searched, and my hand luggage X-rayed. Francois was escorted away by customs officials, and when I reboarded the flight north to San Francisco, he was nowhere to be seen. This was the last occasion I ever saw Francois.

THE BAGMAN'S OM

It had been two years since the Babe's arrest and incarceration. No other individuals had been implicated in the bust, and I had shelved all blotter work. Any revival of my blotter business appeared improbable for the foreseeable future. I turned my attention to Julie's Mediterranean cooking project, something we had been considering for the last year.

America's attitude towards food was undergoing a transformation in the 1980s and this was more than evident in the State of California. Restaurants featuring innovative styles of cooking were sprouting up, and the chalice of the gastronomic avant-garde thought nothing of bringing down the barriers of tradition. Fusion food, the mixing of one or more cuisines, was de rigueur, and both men and women were flocking to cooking classes to extend their gourmand libido. Attending one of Julie's cooking classes was more than just simply learning how to prepare and cook chicken in different styles. Her lessons went beyond the chemistry of the kitchen, incorporating as they did, aspects of history, geography, culture and anthropology. As a teacher of many years, she was able to transform her subject, making it appealing in a modern documentary style. Listening to her narrative on the Souks of Marrakech and the *Plaka* of Athens, you would be transformed into such exotic destinations by her engaging storytelling.

Encouraged by her patrons Julie began researching the feasibility of opening her own cooking school somewhere in the Mediterranean. Early the following year, we travelled back to Greece and the familiar island of Crete. We set out in search of a suitable property that could be adapted for a proposed cooking school. After a week of tireless searching, we stumbled across an old traditional stone house in the Northern village of Koutouloufari. The location was ideal; off the beaten track but within a twenty-minute drive of an upmarket hotel where we could lodge attendees in comfort and style during their stay in Crete. We returned to California and began planning a marketing and promotion strategy for the school's inception the following year. Our financial investment in the project would be substantial, but given the probability of future income from the blotter business, we pressed ahead with the school venture. The eggs were in the basket, but the shells were about to break.

Although Ted's news came as a bolt out of the blue the initial implications did not appear to be a total disaster. Tragically, the Babe's father had suffered a cardiac arrest whilst at home on his coffee plantation in Costa Rica. he had been rushed to a hospital in San Jose; sadly, overnight, he had lapsed into a coma, failed to regain consciousness and passed away.

His assets were held in testate with the Babe as the sole beneficiary. Somewhere concealed securely was a supply of the ET, ergotamine tartrate precursor required for any further LSD synthesis. With Babe languishing behind bars, we would probably need some form of power of attorney before accessing his father's assets. Besides, we had no idea at this point if the Babe even knew the location of the ET stash, and ex-CIA operatives were naturally more secretive than most. There were to be discovered a myriad of false trails, codebooks, false passports, dummy companies, misleading bank accounts, safety-box keys in unknown locations and storage facilities in six different countries. There was a small trust fund from which the Babe could withdraw a regular limited amount of funds whilst incarcerated and the documentation was sealed by his father's attorney until he was released from prison. No point in crying over spilt milk. Ted and I would have to do 'time' along with the Babe.

The sudden and unanticipated loss of additional income meant we would have to seek and find additional investment for the cooking school project. Following a series of classes at a Los Angeles cooking school, Julie returned to San Francisco with the news one of her students would invest the remaining required finance.

In March, refurbishment work began on the property in Crete. A commercial oven and grill arrived from Italy and an outdoor terrace was constructed to accommodate an al fresco dining area. A local carpenter was commissioned to custom-build traditional island furniture and we scoured the island to find Cretan terracotta pottery and tableware. The stainless-steel cooking range was the only compromise made to the authenticity of a Greek island kitchen, and by August, we were ready to open the doors for business. The September arrival date of the first class of students was a double celebration as Julie was now pregnant and expecting our first child in the following Spring. We wintered in San Francisco, and in early April, Julie gave birth to a healthy boy whom we christened Cordell. Junior's timing couldn't have been more providential as the new year's first students were due on Crete in two weeks. With airline regulations preventing newborn infants from flying until they are at least seven days old, we would be cutting it fine, arriving at the school barely four days before the first class. We were technically still illegal aliens, albeit documented, but our eight-day-old son, a United States citizen, sported a brand-new American passport. Perhaps he could nominate us for legal status? Cordell spent most of the flight to Greece via New York plugged into his mother's nipple safely avoiding the risk of permanent hearing impairment that could have been precipitated by any sudden and rapid change in air pressure.

A joint promotion sponsored by the Greek National Tourist Board brought a group of American travel and food writers as part of a junket. I met up with the hacks in the port town and capital, Heraklion and accompanied them on a guided tour of the local food market. A small but industrious market barely one hundred metres long, but inconceivably, three of America's most prestigious travel writers contrived to get themselves lost, and I had to muster a search party. From Heraklion, we drove to the school, a twenty-five-minute coastal drive, where awaiting them, Julie had provided a mouth-watering spread. Over the next six months the school was featured in several newspapers and leading trade publications in the United States.

I had grown restless. The Greek project was primarily Julie's brainchild, and my involvement was minimal. The following year, I stayed behind in San Francisco whilst she and our son journeyed to Crete, where they were to remain for the following eight months. I continued to work on blotter designs, more out of artistic habit than necessity. I began to use computer-generated images using fledgling design applications. Graphic software programs were extremely primitive in the mid-1980s, but the potential of the technology was apparent. It had been almost three years since I last spoke with Ted. After Babe's father's death, he had severed all contact with his Bay Area associates and acquaintances. Out of the blue I received instructions on how to travel north to Oregon. Ted's instructions had been clear enough.

"Take Interstate 5 north to the Oregon border, then old Highway 57 past Madras. Turn right on 293 and Rajneeshpuram is approximately ten miles down the road. Call this number when you arrive in town." I was bewildered. I couldn't believe that a pair of Indian communities, Madras and Rajneeshpuram were also located in Oregon. There was an obvious clue in the latter's name that I had overlooked.

In 1981 a religious whose early followers emanated from the Indian city of Poona had purchased an old ranch property, 'Big Muddy,' outside the town of Antelope in North Central Oregon. They began a redevelopment programme on the site, and within months their flock of disciples had expanded tenfold. Dressed distinctively in orange or red robes the Rajneeshees, named after their spiritual leader, Bhagwan Shree Rajneesh, had incorporated the ranch and outlying properties into their own 'city' and Antelope was renamed Rajneeshpuram. Now outnumbering the original locals, the expanding commune took control of the local school utilities and set up its own police force. The oxymoronically sounding Rajneesh Police force was to use its power to practice control and intimidation over neighbouring communities and stamp out all criticism.

Ted's former wife, the exiled once-Mormon, had returned to the States as a fully-fledged Rajneeshee Sannyasin or commune leader and was now a luminary within the cult. Any close, intimate relationship that she once shared with Ted was a distant memory, but she had gone out of her way to renew her acquaintance with her former husband. Her business proposition required Ted's professional skills as an organic chemist. Having eagerly accepted her offer he relocated to Oregon the previous year.

I was twenty miles outside Of Rajneeshpuram but had already been on the road for twelve hours and needed some rest. I checked into the 'Royal Dutch Motel.' After a sleep I awoke and telephoned Ted. An hour later, a primrose Rolls Royce Silver Cloud pulled up outside my room and out stepped a jubilant Ted accompanied by four smiling and stunningly beautiful women. They couldn't keep their hands off him, alternating stroking his groin. One of the quartet stepped towards me and began seductively rubbing her body against mine. Through her skimpy blouse, I could feel the hardness of her nipples against my chest. Ted referred to the women as his 'Twinkies', a fringe benefit that came with his job. Apparently, several female initiates were employed as hostesses. Their role was to liaise with any visiting press or prying eyes, a task that went beyond the bounds of spin-doctoring! They became known as 'Twinkies' after the snack bar 'Hostess Twinkie'. On our drive to the commune, Ted drew from his pocket and offered me a gelatine capsule of MDMA. I was familiar with the drug but had only tried it once, given freely as it was, as part of the 'entrance fee' at a gay nightclub in Dallas, Texas, five years earlier. By the time we arrived, the drug had kicked in. The feeling of euphoria and loss of inhibition added an extra dimension to the tactile advances of the 'Twinkies.' The appropriately named 'X' I had sampled was a product of Ted's labour. Financed by the cult, he had installed on the ranch a state-of-the-art laboratory and, although primarily involved in the manufacture of MDMA (Methylenedioxymethamphetamine), had managed to keep his interest in the synthesis of LSD. Through a Czech intermediary, he had succeeded in procuring a batch of 'ET' and had synthesized two hundred grammes of pure white crystal.

The acid and a substantial amount of the 'X' ecstasy produced were destined for the European market. The Rajneeshees' priority may have been the quest for Nirvana and enlightenment, but that didn't preclude making a buck! They were firmly in control of a huge underground supply of ecstasy, a drug that was yet to be outlawed by the United States Government. Utilizing the community's state-of-the-art graphic software, I reproduced a simple icon based on the Hindu symbol for truth - The 'OM.' The image was transferred to a floppy disc, and the next day, a courier was on their way to Amsterdam with the liquid acid and artwork. Ted paid me a generous fee and handed over a sample bag of MDMA powder. I was tempted to stay longer but forgoing the obvious delights of commune life in Rajneeshpuram, I headed back to the Bay Area.

Weeks after my departure, the citizens of Wasco County elected to incorporatethe city of Rajneeshpuram. On the day the vote was to take place, hundreds of the county's inhabitants were physically unable to cast their votes owing to a mysterious outbreak of salmonella poisoning. It was later determined that elements amongst the Rajneeshees had deliberately infected the food at numerous local eateries to deter anti-cultists from voting.

In 1985, the Bhagwan claimed that Rajneeshpuram had been usurped by a group of militants who had stockpiled assault weapons and engaged in wire-tapping. Within days, a Federal Government multi-agency investigation into alleged criminal activity was set in motion. Although the Rajneeshee were suspected of involvement in illicit drugs, the authorities failed to uncover any direct evidence. Later that year the Bhagwan, whilst attempting to flee the country, was finally arrested in North Carolina and duly charged with immigration irregularities. In November, following a plea-bargaining agreement he was deported back to India. Ted quietly slipped out of Rajneeshpuram before the Federal investigation got underway. He relocated to the Balearic Island of Ibiza and established Europe's first ecstasy distribution operation.

UNIDENTIFIED FLYING OBJET D' ART

"The Land of Enchantment" - From the depths of the magnificent Carlsbad limestone Caverns to the weathered mesas of the high desert, New Mexico casts a spell over all who visit this scenically stunning state. It's easy to understand why the Hopi, Anasazi and Navajo people look upon this region of the Southwest with such reverence. The paradox is that New Mexico, the second poorest state in the Union, is effectively run and controlled by the United States Defense Department.

Located in the high mesa, barely forty miles from Santa Fe, the former Spanish capital of the New World, lies the mysterious and foreboding town of Los Alamos. In the 1930s, this quiet and unassuming location was the site of a private finishing school for the offspring of wealthy Easterners, a place where academic studies were complemented by rigorous outdoor adventure programmes. The reclusiveness of Los Alamos has remained unchanged over the last sixty years, but today's inhabitants of this now sprawling town are mostly made up of the scientists responsible for the development of America's weapons of mass destruction. Nineteen thousand boffins and their families, living in their own private world. A town where you are more likely to hear German or Hungarian spoken by customers in the local supermarket. An eerie characterless place is full of grey characterless people. A town once visited, never to return. It was at Los Alamos, under the guidance and leadership of the eminent physicist Robert Oppenheimer, that the atomic bomb was developed. Incredibly, there is even a museum dedicated to the pioneering work carried out in the field of nuclear weaponry.

Displayed are original samples of vitrified glass from the first atomic bomb test detonated at *'Trinity'* two hundred miles to the south. Moving chronologically through the archival enlarged photographs from the numerous atom and hydrogen bomb tests, each giant mushroom cloud reaches further out into the stratosphere. Full-colour reproductions of Armageddon. Weaving my way past the life-sized replicas of the two bombs dropped on Japan, Hiroshima's *'Fat Man'* and Nagasaki's *'Little Boy,'* I found the concept of a museum commemorating sanity gone awry chilling and unsettling.

In the southern part of the state lie the majestic gypsum dunes of *'White Sands.'* Fenced off from prying eyes since the 1950s, the Federal government has used this vast natural phenomenon as a missile testing range. The extent of the military's presence is no more apparent than at Albuquerque's international airport, which lies dwarfed in the shadow of Kirtland Air Force Base, home to many of the country's most advanced nuclear-capable bomber squadrons. No wonder there are more recorded UFO sightings in the state of New Mexico than anywhere else on the planet!

The ongoing geographical separation between Julie and myself had put a considerable strain on our relationship and our marriage was beginning to unravel. We agreed on a trial separation and since I needed time away from San Francisco, I drove out of Albuquerque airport and headed north to Santa Fe. I was offered a management position st the newly-opened high-profile restaurant 'The Coyote Cafe.' The establishment had rapidly become one of the country's hottest tickets with eager patrons jetting in from coast to coast.

I was invited to stay with an old friend from San Francisco until I found more permanent accommodation. Bari had taken early retirement from an executive position with United Airlines and spent most of his free time indulging in his passion for fly fishing. Clearly demonstrating my ignorance, I found it difficult to imagine fishing in the desert, but it turned out the state had some of the finest trout streams in the country.

The city of Santa Fe has strict building codes and all new building developments have to be kept in keeping with the traditional Southwestern style. Adobe is the preferred external construction material and buildings are restricted to just three storeys in height. On the surface, you have a sprawling town looking like everybody's quaint and romantic idea of the Wild West where out-of-towners, many of whom have purchased second homes in the area, fall in line with this phoney notion by dressing up as 'Cowboys and Cowgirls' the moment they hit town. Faded jeans, Lucchese boots and Stetson hats and you would think everyone is an extra in a John Ford western movie. Token Native Americans line the sidewalk of the main square hawking fake artefacts manufactured in Taiwan. Keen to promote its image as an Art & Craft community every second store is an 'Art' gallery, invariably filled with garish paintings of 'Indian' chiefs sitting cross-legged and smoking peace pipes. It comes as no surprise to discover that some retired doctor or dentist from Manhattan has churned out these amateurish portraits. Hispanics make up the largest ethnic community but rarely rise above the station of maintenance crew whose job is to keep the town looking 'Oh! So perfect!' for the weekenders. Amongst the remaining diverse populous can be found lesbian communes and a whole spectrum of New Age enthusiasts ranging from crystal worshippers to rebirthing phreaks. (n.b. New Age spelling). I was shocked to discover that I was, in fact, a reincarnation of a Roman Centurion!

The Coyote Cafe had opened its doors for business just in time for the summer tourist onslaught. Thanks to a slick nationwide promotion campaign, the restaurant was packed from day one. Credit the chef/owner Mark Miller who was a master of self=promotion but sadly inept as a line cook in a commercial kitchen. The problem was that Mark worked in first gear, and in an establishment seating over 500 covers per night, he was a liability. Diplomatically, I convinced him that his marketing skills were an even greater asset to the business than his cooking, so he was duly dispatched across the country on a lengthy and extensive promotional campaign. He worked tirelessly, giving TV interviews, cooking demonstrations and making himself available at book-signing events. Whilst he was away clocking up the frequent flyer miles, he left behind a competent kitchen staff that was fast and efficient but still able to replicate his intricate menus. The staff hierarchy for restaurants in America is perhaps no different from any other organization. In the pecking order, the wait staff have the most disposable income garnered from gratuities. After their night shifts, they flaunt their status by throwing away too much money on cocaine; cooks tend to smoke marijuana and drink copious amounts of beer. The Coyote Cafe was an exception to the general rule as most of the cooks had a penchant for organic psychedelics and in particular, magic mushrooms. The problem was this was not an extracurricular activity as, more often than not, they would be intoxicated from the psilocybin during service. No wonder the day-glow plates always appeared so colourful, even to the normal eye.

The restaurant quickly established a glowing (Excuse the pun) reputation for itself, and on any given weekend, the reservation list would look like the 'Who's who of Hollywood cognoscenti.' The spectacular landscapes of the region brought many movie production companies to the area and the town. The young 'brat pack' members, Charlie Sheen, Emilio Estevez, Keifer Sutherland and Lou Diamond Philips, were staying in town whilst shooting a forthcoming Western: 'Young Guns.' Some of the members were regulars at the restaurant, and after hours, we would adjourn to 'Evangelo's' kitsch Hawaiian bar for late-night drinking and pool sessions.

A pre-Christmas party was organized by the sous-chef and held at his property on the road to Santa Fe's ski resort. Guests were greeted with tumblers of homemade punch, and it wasn't long before I and others realized the liquid potion had been liberally laced with LSD. Heavy metal music blasted out of the home stereo system, a style of music I find grating at the best of times. I decided to make an early exit. Three times I tried to drive back to town but on each occasion, I left the driver's seat without even starting the vehicle's ignition. The hallucinations I was experiencing made the thought of driving an impossibility. I waited until sunrise and having watched the nearby silhouetted mesa turn to a deep orange and then a golden yellow I felt sufficiently compos mentis to finally make the drive. I headed downhill to the highway and drove west with the rising sun flooding my rearview mirror. Once safely home I sat up for quite some time absorbed by the rainbows cast from the hanging crystals swaying gently to and fro from the kitchen ceiling.

Time off was a rarity but on one free day my head waiter Johnny and I headed out to 'Madrid'(pronounced MAD-RID) to watch some of the location filming. So, after a marijuana breakfast of blue corn tortillas, we drove out of town to the site. Johnny had recently purchased a brand-new cherry red 4-wheel drive off-road Chevrolet and was eager to test the vehicle's capabilities. Tourists in the region are often warned of the dangers of relatively low amounts of alcohol consumption due to the body's difficulty in acclimatizing to the altitude of 8000 feet. That morning, we completely overlooked that smoking high-grade marijuana posed similar problems. Within fifteen minutes and without a map, we were hopelessly lost and had no sign of civilization as far as the eye could see. Over the next half hour, we crisscrossed a web of dirt tracks, finally descending into an arroyo. We continued following the riverbed until ahead of us stood a thicket of cottonwood beyond the trees, at the bottom of a gully, I could just make out the outline of the roofs of half a dozen buildings. We arrived at a farm gate flanked by six-foot-high razor wire fencing. Appearing from nowhere were suddenly three figures armed with automatic rifles.

A shot was discharged into the air and Johnny slammed on the brakes. A bull dyke warned us off in no uncertain terms confirming we were in a male-free zone. We had stumbled across a militant lesbian compound and the only course of action was to beat a hasty retreat. The truck climbed out of the dried-up riverbed and ahead, less than a hundred yards away, we spotted a Kenilworth pantechnicon moving at speed. We'd spent the previous thirty minutes driving in an arroyo oblivious to the fact that the road we should have been on ran parallel and above us to the right.

I could see why the town of Madrid had been chosen as a film location. Aside from very few motor vehicles, it looked like one had stepped back in time to the frontier days of the 1870s. Even the local saloon had its obligatory drunk Indian or was he from central casting? There were no bottles of liquor on display, which was a pity as I was in the mood for a large Bourbon after our early skirmish with the bull dyke. The only beverage available was warm Budweiser beer as the bar's refrigeration had packed up earlier in the day. After a mouthful of what tasted like mulled ale, I stepped back outside into the searing heat. A single road ran through the town, and by foot, would take less than five minutes from one end to the other. There was a mini-market, a general store that doubled as the post office and the only other store had a set of three balls hanging above its entrance. The sight of the shiny blue Porsche 911, Cadillac Seville and a brand-new off-roader with sparkling alloy wheels seemed incongruous in this backwater. I assumed, incorrectly, that the vehicles were connected to the film production company, but Johnny was quick to put my inquisitive mind at rest.

"Dope dealers! They're probably in town to collect their mail. The Caddy belongs to Ernie Banks. An 'Angel' out of Oakland. Moved out here years ago. Rumour has it he runs the biggest amphetamine operation west of Texas! Apparently, he pumps out shitloads of speed. It's believed he manufactured it in a bathtub on his ranch. The only contact these guys have with the outside world is through a P.O. Box at the post office. No regular mail delivery and no phones. Occasionally, Ernie shows up at 'Evangelo's' to shoot some pool. I'll introduce you to him."

I was barely over the trigger-happy lesbians. The last thing I needed was an introduction to a psycho speed freak Hell's Angel. It's strange how our minds can conjure up negative stereotypical preconceptions. There I was, expecting some sweaty, bare-chested gorilla tattooed from head to toe and dressed in biker gear, when out of the post office stepped a short, balding, middle-aged man in a yellow shirt and gleaming white suit. I couldn't picture him straddled across a Harley Davidson! Besides, his feet would barely touch the peddles.

Johnny was aware of my blotter work, but I was startled when I was introduced to Ernie as:

" The guy who does the acid blotter back in Frisco."

I don't suppose for one minute that Ernie would have been introduced to me as the West's largest speed supplier! Ernie's response was diplomatic but to the point.

"Probably unlikely that your friend wanted that information to be divulged. If so, I am sure he would have preferred the option of choosing the time and place himself?"

Ernie accompanied us to the film set about a mile outside of town. Johnny's unfortunate introduction had aroused Ernie's curiosity, and along the drive, he kept probing me about the subject of blotter. We arrived in time to see the film crew wrapping up for the day. One of the lead actors had gone down with a throat infection and the shooting was curtailed. The production crew would soon be on their way back to Santa Fe. We dropped Ernie back in Madrid and kept strictly to the highway on the drive home.

During the Winter months, the town goes into hibernation. Only the die-hard skiing fraternity passed through and many of the businesses that were dependent on tourism closed down for three months. The Coyote Cafe's business was down by 50% but the restaurant remained open seven nights a week. 'Evangelo's, the local hangout was less than a block away and was my usual last stop before heading home. The dilapidated ground-floor bar featured three leatherette banquettes and a decor of plastic Hawaiian garlands spiralling around fibreglass Polynesian totem poles. The theme didn't exactly gel with its Greek name or its Guatemalan proprietor, Jose Lindor. I was on my second and final margarita when I went into the bar strolled Ernie Banks. He wasn't there for the pool game! He was looking for enough blotter for one million hits. He had acquired a substantial amount of liquid LSD some years before in exchange for other goods and services. I put a call into Ted, who had recently returned from Ibiza to the Bay Area following another major altercation with his ex-wife over the ecstasy affair. That amount of acid doesn't go unnoticed, and Ted's conclusion that it was connected to the 'Brotherhood' in Southern California, perhaps in exchange for a batch of methamphetamine. I had to be sure that the mysterious Mr. Banks wasn't a DEA or undercover Federal operative. I decided to run a check on him, starting with his vehicle registration.

Ailai, an attractive woman in her early forties and with a wild carefree spirit, headed the State of New Mexico's native American substance abuse programme. In addition to her many talents, she also had a line on the best dope I had encountered since arriving in town. Her professional role put her in touch with the local native American tribal leaders, and through these contacts, I was privileged to be one of the few non-natives to witness the peyote-induced and rarely seen tribal snake dance. The ceremony involved the consumption of the hallucinogenic cactus plant followed by a twenty-four-hour dance marathon in which the participants performed closely with a collection of deadly snakes: not exactly for the faint-hearted. I was fascinated by the inter-action of the participants with their limbless reptilian partners. Was it the effects of the Peyote that induced this synergy? I've witnessed snake charmers in India and the Jemma el-Fina market square in Marrakech, but the understanding between the Hopi tribesmen and the venomous snakes was something to behold. Many of the Hopi I spoke with explained that the animal names bestowed on them were a direct result of individual peyote encounters.

Over lunch, I asked Ailai for help running a check on Ernie. I liked her straightforwardness, and she consented to help without any questions. Her position within the New Mexico State government undoubtedly meant it would be relatively easy to source the information I needed through the State's DMV (Department of Motor Vehicles). I invited her for dinner that evening, but with a smile and a gleam in her eyes, she suggested we dine at her place. Before the meal, Ailai passed me an envelope containing the following information:

"*Ernest Borgmester.*" Born November 17, 1936. New Mexico License-holder since 1974. Address: P.O. Box 216, Madrid, New Mexico 87501.

We had previously agreed to meet at the vegetable section at the local 'Safeways.' I've always been one of those inquisitive types who tries to build up a profile of fellow shoppers based on the contents of their shopping trolleys. Ernie's cart was stocked with a large economy pack of frozen Chinese dinners, a gallon jug of Jack Daniels Whiskey, a case of coke, two large jars of coffee granules, a carton of Pall Mall cigarettes and a copy of the weekly TV guide. From my observation, I determined that Ernie was probably a loner who wiled away his evenings glued to the TV with a micro-waved meal and a stiff glass of bourbon close to hand. I tossed the A4 envelope containing the blotter design into his shopping trolley

We were in the 'Land of Enchantment,' the birthplace of Ufology, the home of the famous Rosewall incident, and the site of numerous alien sightings. A month later, a postal delivery company dropped off four large boxes containing perforated sheets of a flying saucer addressed to P.O. Box 216 at the Madrid post office.

BACK TO BLIGHTY

Six months had passed since Julie and I had separated, and she and our son were now living back in the UK in Somerset. I had fulfilled my contract with the Coyote Cafe, and to be closer to Cordell, I took up an option of a consultancy in London. Twelve years had passed since leaving England. Over that time, I endured the two terms of Ronnie 'The Gipper' Reagan's Presidency. The only mild consolation was I had missed the tenure of the UK's Prime Minister who lacked taste in women's handbags. During my self-imposed exile the standard of living in London arose appreciably. All the ostentation and trappings of the nouveau riche were plain to be seen, but people had become self-centred, hard and less-caring.

It was a boom time, and investors were finding numerous frivolous ways of disposing of their wealth. London was about to embark on a gastronomic revolution not too dissimilar from that I had experienced in America in the early 1980s. Even members of the Royal Family were getting in on the act, and Lord Lindley and Patrick Litchfield's first venture was to be 'Deals', A pseudo-American restaurant located in West London's newly-developed Chelsea Harbour. My professional experience in the 'Colony' dovetailed with their plans and I was brought on board to get the project off the ground. Apart from the young Lindley's production of the original wooden banquettes the involvement of the two Lords was peripheral. Pre-opening parties were like the 'A' list from Debrett's peerage. Ageing duchesses, marquises and barons from the far corners of the realm tucked heartedly into hamburgers and fries in homage to their entrepreneurial relatives. Princesses Margaret, Diana and the Duchess of York made guest appearances accompanied by the familiar coterie of Metropolitan Police

Protection officers who paced nervously, giving a new twist to the restaurant's ambience.

I was a week away from completing my stint at 'Deals' when Johnny called me from Santa Fe. Ernie had found a buyer for his acid and wanted me to fly out and dip his consignment. My sister, a longtime London resident, was going through a difficult patch in her marriage, so I invited her husband, Sean, to join me on the trip to New Mexico. The visit got off to an inauspicious start at the customs desk in St. Louis, our first point of entry into the United States. As a gift for Johnny, I had packed four bottles of Czech Budweiser Budvar, the original Budweiser beer. Trying to convince any patriotic American that one of his country's greatest cultural icons was usurped from the former Communist country, The Czech Republic (Since renamed Czechia) was not a simple matter. The customs official went through the standard routine regarding the importation of plants, animals or certain food products, but having opened my carry-on bag, he discovered the infamous beer. I made a valiant attempt to re-educate the customs official on the history of

Budweiser beer, but there we were, in the city of St. Louis, home of America's most famous brewery, Budweiser! The 'fake' bottles were confiscated, and I was reprimanded for attempting to discredit an important paradigm of his country's great heritage. I was finally allowed to catch my connecting flight to Albuquerque.

Ernie had done his homework. A quantitative analysis of the liquid LSD revealed a concentration of 26.13 grams of Lysergic Acid Diethylamide in 1000ml.aqueous solution with a potential yield of 261,300 hits of 100-microgram acid. What remained uncertain was the quality of the product. I apologized to Johnny for not being able to provide him with the Czech beer but hoped the sample LSD might prove more enticing. We headed over to Evangelo's to shoot some pool. We were in the middle of the first game when Johnny began commenting on the electric blue vapour trails emanating from the balls as they careened around the table. I set up shop in a sculptor friend's studio who was away for the weekend in Los Angeles and got straight down to work. I closed the studio's blinds, unrolled the black plastic bin-liners and laid them side by side across the floor. I transferred the liquid LSD to a five-litre glass round fishbowl and carefully added a precise amount of Stolichnaya 100-proof vodka, stirring the mixture thoroughly. In the past, I have often used Methanol as a solvent, which is quick-drying, but with large quantities, Methanol is problematic as rapid evaporation can dramatically reduce the quantity of the finished product. Utilizing a rectal hypodermic, I transferred a measured amount of blended solution to a glass baking dish in which I had laid the first sheet of blotter. As the acid hit the paper's surface it immediately began spreading out until the entire sheet was saturated. I removed the sheet from the tray and laid it out carefully at one end of the carpet of bin liners. Thirteen hours later, I laid the final piece of blotter. I killed the studio lights and, using a pocket ultra-violet lamp, scanned the entire 261 sheets of paper. There was the odd blemish, which I touched up with a squirt from a glass eyedropper. My calculations had been precise, and I felt a sense of professional pride when I measured the residual acid, which totalled 8 ml of the solution! I set an alarm clock and settled down for a nap. Once awake I collected the dried sheets of blotter, batched them, wrapped them in plastic saran wrap and loaded them into a brown paper bag. On my way to the car, I tossed the empty vodka bottles, syringe, baking tray and plastic liners into a garbage dumpster and drove away.

I had dropped off Sean, my sister's husband, at the hotel where we were staying. On my return, I apologized for abandoning him so soon after our arrival. He assured me that he had been perfectly content amusing himself with the remote control and the access it gave to sixty TV channels. When I walked in, he was glued to the Weather Channel. There was currently a monsoon downpour in Jakarta, Indonesia, with a temperature of 98 degrees Fahrenheit.

Johnny's girlfriend Karen opened the front door, shaking her head in disgust.

"You'd better go in and see for yourself. He's in the bedroom."

It looked like I had come face-to-face with a Nazi concentration camp victim. Johnny, wide-eyed, was sitting bolt upright in the bed. Gone were his flowing locks. All that remained was an irregular-shaped stubble and balding patches where the hair had been crudely shaved. He had earlier convinced himself that his body was crawling with iridescent red centipedes. He had sat naked in the bath whilst struggling to cleanse himself of the imagined arthropods. In desperation, he had resorted to shaving his head in a final attempt to rid himself of the perceived threat. Initially, there had been bright moments during his trip, but one thing was certain, and that was the strength of the dose was more than sufficient!

The following morning, I drove to a pre-arranged meeting at a shopping mall car park. I shook hands with Ernie and loaded the brown bag into the Cadillac's trunk. I collected Sean from the hotel, and we set off west to Arizona for a drive through Monument Valley. I repeatedly apologized for my lengthy absence with a flimsy story of meeting up with an old flame. He seemed unconcerned as he had discovered the pay-per-view porn channels.

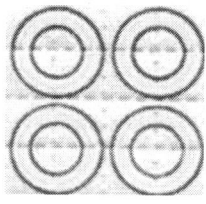

IN - HOUSE DIVERSIONS

Following Sean's return to England in August, I stayed in Santa Fe until October before flying to New York where I was to meet up with my sister. Amanda had established herself in the world of fashion and had been instrumental in procuring financial backing for the up-and-coming English designer John Galliano. She was currently the personal assistant for another fashion rising star, Alistair Blair. The industry's annual autumn circus had touched down in New York just in time for Halloween, an occasion that might be more than interesting with the added ingredient of a bag of psilocybin mushrooms that I had received from Ernie as a going-away gift. From La Guardia airport, I took a cab into Manhattan, arriving at the offices of the public relations company Brandstetter and Johnson. I strolled into the spacious 17th-floor office suite where the visiting UK entourage was already on its third round of martinis. Two cocktails later, a group of us headed out to a Tribeca trattoria, where I took the opportunity to liberally lace our black truffle pasta course with the magic mushrooms.

Susan Barsch, a famed London party-thrower, had relocated to New York, and that evening, her Halloween extravaganza was being held at an uptown nightclub. With my feet appearing not to touch the ground, I surfed down the broad curved staircase to the dance floor below. I glided to a halt face-to-face with a young man scantily dressed in a gold lame thong accompanied by a writhing six-foot boa constrictor wrapped appropriately around his neck. I declined an offer to have the snake's forked tongue plunged down my throat. It was undoubtedly a colourful occasion, not solely due to the mushrooms. Following a brief detour to a house party, we finally ended up back where we had started, the PR company headquarters, at seven in the morning. Probably due to her discombobulated state, my sister had completely forgotten the hotel in which she was staying, so I ended up laying out the Alistair Blair Autumn cashmere collection on the office floor as emergency bedding and fell asleep.

The office phone rang incessantly. I finally staggered to my feet and answered the building concierge's call. The head buyers for the department stores, Barneys and Macys, were waiting in the lobby. Amanda hastened to the bathroom and slapped on some makeup while I offered the buyers coffee and small talk. Heaven knows who they thought I was, although the English accent suggested I must have had something to do with the sales force. A secretary wearing oversized sunglasses tip-toed past and was press-ganged into ironing the cashmere 'bedding.'

Hundreds of thousands of dollars in sales would be spent that day, and the future careers of many young designers were in the balance. Mission miraculously accompanied my sister and I headed to Katz's deli for a full Jewish breakfast.

My sister, Amanda, has always prided herself on having her finger on the pulse of London's club nightlife. Leicester Square's 'The Cafe De Paris' had recently become her venue of choice, where every Wednesday evening, the fashion and entertainment crowd would gather to network and socialize. The nightclub had originally opened in the 1920s, and tragically, 34 people died from a German bomb during World War 11. However, like Phoenix rising literally from the ashes, the club reopened as a theatre club hosting such luminaries as Frank Sinatra, Judy Garland, Humphrey Bogart and Lauren Bacall. In the 1980s, my good friend Nick Fry had resurrected the venue in the style of a French cabaret club, but as the decade was closing, a new infectious style of music was infiltrating the London club scene.

The roots of 'House Music' can be traced back to Chicago in the mid-1980s, but it was a group of English DJs returning from Ibiza that really led to the music's UK development. The missing ingredient was the now commonplace party drug 'ecstasy.' Knowing of Ted the chemist's relocation to Ibiza, it came as no surprise to hear of the English DJ's drug-fuelled weekend on the party island. On a chilly Thursday morning, we arrived at Heathrow airport. Rather than trying to shake off the effects of jet lag, Amanda was already psyching herself up for a night of revelry at the Mayfair nightclub, *Legends*' Under the banner of MFI (Mad for it!), club runners Spike and Neville were hosting London's hottest Thursday night party.

It was just before 11 pm and a large swarm of partygoers had already gathered outside *'Legends.'* The obligatory bouncers barred the entrance and an attractive fashion agency booker armed with a pen and clipboard was supervising the VIP guest list. The dread-locked Neville spotted my sister waved the formality of the entrance fee ushered us through the door and escorted us to the bar. The club was already packed. A futuristic stainless-steel staircase spiralled down to a rectangular dance floor whilst the DJ, Judge Jules, was seamlessly mixing one track into another. There was a repetitive uniformity to the rhythm, a basic four beats to the bar that reverberated through the sound system's bass speakers. Dancers, their arms extended upward, bodies gyrating to the music's beat were dressed in an array of lurid casual clothing. T-shirts sporting bright yellow 'smiley' faces, logos of American baseball caps representing the New York Yankees, LA Dodgers, and every other major league team and an assortment of sports footwear. The club's walls were decorated with black light imagery fluorescing under the flashing ultra-violet lighting.

Amanda popped a gelatine capsule containing a white powder into my mouth. Within half an hour, it became impossible to remain motionless. The relentless driving beat of the shaman on the turntables drove the crowd to a higher level of euphoria. I glanced at the dance floor and quickly realized that the combination of music and ecstasy was the catalyst that had led to the communal trance-like state. Complete strangers were coming up to me smiling, hugging and in some cases, embracing me. Apart from a gregarious nature, eveyone shared one physical trait. Their pupils were severely dilated. I remembered fondly the time briefly spent at the Rajneesh commune in Oregon and the Bhagwan's MDMA-induced followers.

The synergy of drugs and music was hypnotic, and my body remained riveted to the dance floor. The country was in the last throws of Thatcherism and the somewhat dillusioned youth seemed primed for a cultural transformation. MDMA, or ecstasy as it was commonly named, had been the drug of choice amongst America's gay community since the late 1970s but had failed to become mainstream. I finally made my way back up the staircase to the bar. Needing to rehydrate, I ordered a beer, the taste of which I found disgusting. I looked around and noticed most of the revellers were drinking bottled water. The bad taste of the beer lingered, so I ordered a glass of water. I was charged £2.50, which I was told was to compensate for the fact that hardly anyone was ordering alcohol.

Three-thirty a.m. arrived, and the closing anthem, William Pitt's '*City Lights*', brought the night to an end. Or so I thought. MFI was just the hors d' oeuvres and the main course was just about to be served up. The enterprising club promoters, Spike and Neville, had taken over a photographic studio in North London, and the party had simply relocated. I arrived in the cab, paid the driver and hastened into the studio. The same DJ was already spinning a string of 'house' anthems and the floor was crammed with furious ravers. The ecstasy dealer had installed himself at the end of a make-shift bar and there was a queue for his services. I sat down by the side of the DJ engrossed in the skill of his music selection and mixing. Like some mystical Pied Piper, he had the audience in the palm of his hand.

The following afternoon, whilst the music was still reverberating through my brain, I headed off to Soho to a dance music record store. The store was packed with house music aficionados eagerly snapping up copies of the latest vinyl 12-inch releases. I had no idea of the artists or tune's titles from the previous night. I hummed a few bars or lines from lyrics, and within ten minutes, I'd bought a stack of records. What impressed me the most was the sales assistant's ability to identify a track from my feeble intonations. Naturally, he turned out to be a DJ, and we arranged to meet the following week at MFI in Mayfair.

I had first met Tim Hudson at the doomed St. James restaurant back in 1976. He had relocated to the Bay Area from New York but hailed from Chicago. We had remained in touch and he was back on home turf in the 'Windy City'. At the time Julie was still in Greece so I travelled to Illinois to spend a few days with Tim. I hadn't been in Chicago for many years and was looking forward to catching a live performance by one of the city's legendary blues stars who used to play regularly in the local bars and clubs. Unfortunately, I was too late, as many of the surviving practitioners of this very American genre, the Blues, had either succumbed to old age or died. Most of the old clubs were gone, replaced by disco music. After copious flaming sambucas, we ended up at the 'Music Box' around 3 am. just as the DJ Ron Hardy was getting into a groove. Venues such as this, 'The Warehouse' and 'The Power Plant' were the crucibles from which house music first appeared. A genre of music that everyone believed would be long gone but has survived to today, 40 years later! Tim had scored some MDA and acid, and we spent the night 'candy flipping' to one of the godfathers of house music.

The roots of England's acid house music movement may have sprouted forth from Chicago, but if it wasn't for those English DJs and their wild weekend in Ibiza, things might have been different. Influenced by a musical amalgam of disco, Euro dance, Balearic beats and house, clubs popped up all over England. Ecstasy production and distribution increased dramatically. The drug was flooding the UK. One of the country's established shoe designers was caught by customs with a stash at Heathrow, but influential individuals interceded, and he escaped with caution. The authorities, desperate to stem the tide, hurriedly upgraded MDMA (ecstasy) to a class 'A' category, aligning it with heroin, cocaine, magic mushrooms and LSD.

The weekend came around again, and I met up with the DJ/sales assistant from the Soho store. The rapid advance of musical electronics had brought the sampler to the high street. 'Any kid with basic equipment could sample, loop, dub and record his tracks from his bedroom on high-quality digital audio tape and, for an outlay of a few pounds, could press fifty or a hundred copies of his 12-inch vinyl record. No expense for designed labelling was necessary. A plain white label with the title or artist's name could be hand-written with a ballpoint pen. In some cases, these 'white label' records became in demand and were rare because of their limited pressing. Through the conduit of music, club culture was exploding throughout the United Kingdom, influencing not only musical tastes but the fashion industry, design and contemporary art.

At MFI, a nucleus of partygoers developed and continued relentlessly through the weekend to early Monday morning. A talented jewelry designer from Merano, Italy, a Korean entrepreneur from Tokyo, a fashion designer from Portugal and a businessman from Cape Town, South Africa joined a West London crowd including The Clash's Mick Jones, newly-converted from his punk persona on an extended continuous ecstasy-fuelled hedonistic binge. Maybe I was lucky? I never seemed to suffer from any sort of hangover or bad comedown, but on reflection, I never took any substance other than quality ecstasy or LSD. I barely drank alcohol, and my immediate course of action after a weekend was to refuel with a hearty breakfast and a balanced diet of fruit and vegetables. I put my survival to my current age down to never succumbing to junk food and eating healthily. Perhaps I owe my longevity to Julie's persistent Mediterranean diet, which I have remained faithful to for the last 45 years.

An all-night New Year's Eve bash brought 1989 to a tumultuous close but I was coming close to burnout and needed some time away from the madness. I set off for India. From Delhi, I took a train to Rajasthan province, where I could afford some luxury whilst staying in the former Maharajah's palaces in Jaipur and Udaipur. I journeyed south to Bombay (Since renamed Mumbai) and then to the former Portuguese colony of Goa. Incorporated into the Indian Republic in the 1960s, the state still retained some architectural and cultural heritage from its former European master, but the major Western influence, still intact, was the hippie movement that had imposed its own brand of colonialism over the previous twenty years. Revellers were no longer tripping out to 'Pink Floyd'. House music had already filtered down to the Asian subcontinent and massive full moon parties and rav.es were commonplace. I was close to temptation but retreated to a northern-located beach resort for some serious rest and relaxation. Indulging in fresh coconut milk drinks and searing hot fish curries, my vacation wasn't totally drug-free, having bought a small block of hashish from a cab driver in Mumbai.

I continued to Jordan without incident. At the southern port of Aqaba, I had the bartender of the beach hotel play a cassette of mixed house music. Within minutes, Arabs and their veiled wives were dancing on the beach. In its unstoppable drive to conquer the world house music had infected Jordan! I caught a ferry to the Egyptian Sinai and by bus, went to Cairo, checking into a Giza hotel where, upon opening the room's shutters, I discovered the Great Pyramid before my very eyes. On the trip, I managed to take in three of the most remarkable man-made structures from the past. The Taj Mahal, The Nabataean ruins of Petra and finally, the Pyramids of Giza. I tossed the hashish out of the taxi's window on the way to the airport and the flight back to London.

House music and its many offshoots may have swept through Europe and penetrated Goa and Jordan but the genre was yet to make serious inroads within the wider United States. The time was ripe for a musical recolonization.

GO WEST

I was about to board a flight to Reno, Nevada, where I had the offer to consult on a restaurant project when Ted called. The Babe had been released after spending ten years behind bars. I cancelled my flight and flew to San Francisco for a reunion with my old friends. Before anything else, The Babe was to travel to Costa Rica to unravel the mysteries of his father's estate and, more importantly, the location of the ET, ergotamine tartrate. I hired a car and drove across the Sierras and down into Reno. The arched neon sign stretching across Virginia Street proclaims Reno to be:

"The Greatest Little City in the World."

The reality is that it's nothing more than a poor man's Las Vegas. A blue-collar gambling town. I had an offer to transform the 'El Dorado Casino's flagship Italian restaurant 'La Strada' into a modern Trattoria. The trouble with so many American second, third and fourth generation Italians is that their idea of Italian food is based on obscure grandma village recipes from the nineteenth century. In many cases dishes that would never be seen on a menu in Rome, Florence or any other gastronomic region of the 'mother' country. I admired the casino's concept of focusing on food rather than lavish entertainment for their punters, but in retrospect, I would rather have an hour of Adele or Elton John than a dish of soggy pasta! Unless you wish to indulge a masochistic tendency of fritting away your hard-earned cash gambling, then Reno has very little to offer.

My enthusiasm for house music was beginning to rub off on a long-standing friend, Colette, who I had known since the late 1970s when I bought my first pair of Charles Jourdan shoes from her whilst she was employed at Macy's San Francisco store. We agreed that California specifically San Francisco would be an ideal springboard to promote the new English music and dance craze. Together we outlined plans to bring a production to the state the following summer. In the meantime, The Babe was taking a well-earned rest and would not return from Costa Rica until the new year. I put together a series of possible blotter designs, which I left in Ted's safe care and prepared to fly back to the UK to spend the Winter in London.

Before my departure, I decided to witness, firsthand, the perennial underachieving San Francisco Giants baseball team take on its neighbour the 'Oakland Athletics' in what was billed as the 'Bay Bridge World Series' The bridge, a seven mile-long part cantilever, part suspension structure serves as a trans-Bay road link between the two cities. I was seated twenty rows up and behind home plate in Candlestick Park. The US Marine colour guard had taken up their position, and Nell Carter had completed her rendering of the National Anthem.

The legendary Willie Mays was about to throw the ceremonial first pitch when the ballpark swayed violently from side to side. I've heard tales of near-death experiences but collectively 60.000 people must have felt they were about to die. A major earthquake had struck the city of San Francisco. Once the temblor ceased, to my amazement, there was complete calm amongst the crowd of spectators. People began filing out of the stadium in an orderly fashion although a sense of communal shock was apparent. The distant memory of my Tokyo earthquake experience came flooding back. The Bay Bridge, the symbolic link between San Francisco and Oakland was severed when a section of the westbound roadway collapsed onto the eastern road that ran beneath. Miraculously, no fatalities suffered from the bridge's collapse but if the two local baseball teams had not been involved in the World Series, traffic for that time of the day would have been heavy and the consequences incalculable.

Somewhat shell-shocked, I returned to London for the Christmas holidays. New Year's Eve was spent at a Neville and Spike extravaganza which had now become a regular annual event. I must have been in a convivial mood as a dozen or so revellers turned up at my house. Over the next forty-eight hours the numbers waxed and waned: new faces appearing hourly. Most seemed in various states of pharmaceutical diversions. Not wishing to bring the festivities to an end but needing a break, I packed an overnight bag, headed out to Heathrow airport and boarded a flight to San Francisco. I left the house in Neville's safekeeping, relying on his integrity and the genuine collective responsibility of the party goers. The trip to California wasn't exactly a spur-of-the-moment idea as I needed to reconnoitre for a suitable venue to stage the proposed House Music events. I had called ahead, and, on my arrival, Colette was at the airport to meet me. We spent the evening checking out the largest appropriate venues. We needed somewhere that could accommodate up to fifteen hundred people to cover the additional travel costs of bringing three DJs over from the UK. Not wishing to draw unnecessary attention from the local police and fire department would require a legitimate venue. The appropriately named 'Pleasuredome,' a converted warehouse in the SOMA district (South of Market St.), suited our requirements perfectly. Configured into a giant figure-of-eight, the facility boasted state-of-the-art lighting, an ear-splitting sound system and a fully equipped DJ booth. Contracts were drawn up and signed and the first show was scheduled for Saturday August 19th, 1990. Buoyed with how events had progressed so smoothly and rapidly Colette and I headed off to a neighbourhood bar.

There was one of those rare moments of magnetic attraction between the bartender, Lindy and me. After closing we drove across town to her ground-floor apartment and whiled away the next hour in an outdoor hot tub and jacuzzi. After our weekend together I ended up having to sprint to the departure gate to catch the return flight to London. Whilst in San Francisco, I had intended to speak directly to Ted regarding The Babe's progress in locating the missing ET, but my chance encounter with Lindy had overridden such matters. I arrived back home more jaded than when I had left. On reaching the house I discovered that a group of die-hards were still partying in the basement. Remarkably, except for the breakfast room, the house had been cleaned throughout. The stack of empty bottles revealed that even the Advocaat and cooking sherry had not survived, but to 'celebrate' my return, one of the remaining guests rushed to the nearest off-licence, returning shortly with a six-pack of 'Champagne Rose.' Class! By Monday evening and almost a week to the day, silence finally descended on the household. I crawled into bed and slept for eighteen hours.

Substantial quantities of blotter were starting to infiltrate the underground House scene. With prices of ecstasy varying from £15 to £20 per dose, ravers were already seeking out cheaper alternative pharmaceuticals to sustain them through the night. Paper with a 'Batman & Joker' motif, which appeared on the market to coincide with the release of the Hollywood movie production, was the most commonly available in the UK although examples of the Dutch-produced 'Gorbachev' drifted across the North Sea from Amsterdam. For the hardcore multiple-consumption crowd, it became more economical to 'candy flip' ecstasy and LSD as repeated doses of ecstasy became unnecessary. Perhaps a perverse form of belt-tightening the UK was soon hit by a massive economic turndown and a deep recession.

March arrived, and I prepared to move back to San Francisco to jump-start the promotion campaign for the summer House performances. A second date had been added to the 'Pleasuredome'and my partner Colette was in discussions with a Los Angeles promotor about bringing '*House Nation*,' our working title for the production, to Southern California. We considered the concept of hitting the road with a 'House Music Magic Bu's touring around the Western United States composed of thirty hardcore ravers and DJs aping Ken Kesey's Merry Pranksters from the 1960s. This was, after all, a music revolution sparked by a psychedelic revival. Heading from town to town playing impromptu gigs whilst preaching the gospel of House and rave culture.

Somewhat wisely, the idea was shelved when someone pointed out that outside the major cosmopolitan urban areas, California is primarily a rural conservative state. Unconventional activities by an oddball collection of ecstasy and LSD-fuelled dance freaks would probably induce a sharp response from law enforcement agents.

The synergy of psychedelics with 'House' was primarily what had made club culture so successful in the UK and had rapidly spread across Europe. For the 'House Nation' shows, a readily available supply of Ecstasy and LSD was essential. The Babe had returned from successfully locating the hidden cache of ET (Ergotamine Tartrate), which frustratingly had been stored right under our noses in a Mission District lock-up. He and Ted had already synthesized a sizable batch of LSD and our resourceful chemist had 'recovered' a consignment of Sannyasin ecstasy that had remained undetected from the 1985 Rajneeshpuram fiasco. Neither of them had any idea what rave culture was all about, but they were now totally committed to kick-starting LSD production and distribution. Ted, unable to acquire a sufficient supply of the precursor safrole, had forsaken ecstasy production completely.

I had chosen the three London-based DJs, Judge Jules, Eren and Ricky Morrison as the emissaries best skilled to showcase 'House Nation.' Each had his distinctive style and collectively, their music embraced the most common forms of House music at the time. Eren's sets were a raw, funky underground sound, Ricky's a smooth R&B New Jersey Gospel style, whilst Jules could play just about anything and make it fit any groove. All three were consummate masters of mixing. Jules' additional asset was that he was more outgoing, articulate and ideally suited to best convey to the media the phenomenon of 'House' In addition to press interviews, a two-hour radio slot was arranged with the University of San Francisco's radio station KUSF, the only local station on the cutting edge of youth culture at that time.

Two weeks before the first San Francisco show, Ricky Morrison pulled the plug. He would be willing to fly out and play but wanted a higher fee than we had originally agreed. I was more than just disappointed as I had been instrumental in jump-starting his career as a DJ. I considered his demands unreasonable; however, suddenly, one of the advertised DJS would not be performing. I spoke briefly with a representative of another London-based DJ, Paul Oakenfold, who was currently in Los Angeles remixing the 'Happy Mondays.' Although keen to join the 'House Nation' cast, his newly elevated status as DJ/record producer meant his financial demands unfortunately exceeded our budget.

Colette and I were on our way to the airport to catch a flight down to Los Angeles. An entourage from Manchester's 'Hacienda' nightclub was staging a revue at a Hollywood ballroom, which included club DJs and live performances from the 'Happy Mondays.' I was interested in gauging the response from the audience as the musical style was similar to our forthcoming events. Before leaving the city and heading out to the airport, we stopped at a neighbourhood bar for a cocktail. Colette was always uncomfortable flying and needed to steady her nerves. I was drawn to the music playing over the bar's PA system and enquired with the bartender who was responsible for the mixed tape. The husky-voiced woman replied that it was one of her own recordings, and we had found the DJ who would play the opening set at our shows.

Although well-attended, the LA Manchester show was a real disappointment. The ballrooms' acoustics were dire, the sound system inadequate and the Happy Mondays so strung out on drugs that they had great difficulty remembering their own songs. The mainly white, middle-class Hollywood crowd were obviously familiar with the latest UK fashion magazines, attired as they were in modish dance gear, but they behaved like preening peacocks with the music providing backing for their performances. Only a group of ex-pats were responding to the efforts of the DJ Mike Pickering to stir the crowd. Colette was beginning to have reservations over our shows but I assured her we had the music, the sound system and a more than adequate supply of psychedelics that I intended to distribute liberally to guests as they entered the 'Pleasuredome.' I suppose it was possible that, like some fine wines, this very British experience might fail to make a successful Trans-Atlantic crossing and turn sour, but I at least was intent on enjoying myself.

Oliver Stone's latest movie, a cinematographic biography of the brief but tumultuous career of the legendary 1960s rock band 'The Doors' had just opened in America. Most of the interior concert sequences had been shot on location at San Francisco's 'Warfield Theater' and eager to capture the atmosphere of that era, Stone had hired the services of a company whose unique and psychedelic light show had been an integral part of the Sixties music scene. I managed to track down the ageing hippies who agreed to rig their lighting for our performance at the 'Pleasuredome.' I also augmented the club's sound system with part of the Grateful Dead's PA system. We sound-checked the auditorium, and the whole structure began vibrating.

Six days before the first show, Eren flew into San Francisco accompanied by my friend and club-runner Neville, who had flown out to give moral support to our Californian venture. Jules, a self-confessed workaholic, had prior DJ commitments in England and would not be arriving before the weekend. The local newspapers, 'Chronicle' and 'Examiner' gave us plugs in their mid-week music columns and Colette and I swamped the city with 'House Nation' music flyers. There was nothing more to do than let the clock run down until the doors opened on Saturday evening. I collected Jules from the airport on Friday afternoon. He looked shattered having DJed an all-nighter before flying out that morning. He promptly went to bed and slept until the next morning. I offered him a guided tour of the city, but typical of a DJ, all he wanted was to visit the dance music record stores.

By 8.30 that evening, there was a line of punters stretching a hundred yards outside the 'Pleasuredome' DJ Nikki, our fortuitous discovery, began the evening, and by the time Eren took over the turntables, the dance floor was packed. Although the event was clearly heading for a great success, I had to prise Colette away from her duties in the box office. A sample of Ted's Sannyasin ecstasy and she was soon on the dance floor mesmerized by the music's beat. Mark, a friend of Eren's and regular raver at London's Sunday nightclub 'Solaris' showed up out of the blue and was soon in search of some pharmaceutical stimulation. Jules and Eren played alternating sets with partygoers streaming up to the DJ booth, complementing the two on their music selection. That is interesting considering hardly anyone had heard any of the music before that evening. By 5 a.m., the club's owners wanted to bring the night to a close, but the crowd refused to allow the DJs to stop, and the place rocked for another hour.

Somewhat bleary-eyed, I drove the DJs out, late Sunday afternoon, to the studio of KUSF, where we were to present a two-hour radio seminar and introduction to house music. Our host, a well-known and established Bay Area music critic, was astonished to discover the extent of the cutting-edge musical genre. In addition to domestic tracks from Chicago, Detroit, New Jersey and New York, the listeners were introduced to novel music productions from England, Spain, Italy, Belgium, Germany and Austria. Jules' performance was a revelation. He was natural and had taken to radio like a duck to water. It came as no surprise to me that he went on to become not just one of the World's top club performers but an outstanding ambassador for dance music on the radio. That evening he was winging his way back to London. Johnny, the LSD guinea pig in Santa Fe, had arranged a gig for Eren at a local club for the following Friday, and I had secured a booking at the Mayan Theater in downtown LA a day later. We had three days to kill so I suggested taking a leisurely drive across the Nevada desert to Las Vegas. Always in the footsteps of the intrepid Hunter S. Thompson, this is an interesting place to enjoy an acid trip, if nothing else.

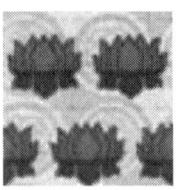

RUNNIN' REBELS

In a normal frame of mind, I have always found Las Vegas repulsive, but in a chemically induced altered state, the desert 'City of Dreams' gives Disneyland a run for its money. An oasis of garish-ersatz reality seems quite sane under the influence of LSD. As our car crested a ridge and the sprawl of Las Vegas, silhouetted by the rising sun, came into view, the hallucinatory effects began to take hold. On the journey downtown, we dropped Neville off at the Excalibur Casino as he had suddenly and urgently been drawn to the tables and a game of Texas Hold 'Em poker. I suggested to him that under the effects of the LSD, he might have difficulty counting the dots on the cards, but he seemed totally confident he was about to make a killing at the tables. Eren sought more exotic entertainment, although I completely misinterpreted his definition of 'exotic', having recommended he should check out the dawn trapeze performance at 'Circus Circus.' It was already seventy-five degrees Fahrenheit. By noon it would soar past the hundred mark. I yearned for a motel with a swimming pool, whilst Colette was prepared to settle on just the room as long as there was a glass-top table to cut and chop her remaining stash of cocaine. For the next few hours, we separated and went our own way.

Several hours later Neville staggered into my room complaining that he hadn't been dealt a winning hand during his entire time at the casino. He'd suffered a protracted loss of just two hundred dollars, which, given his condition, amounted to a 'Win.' Colette had used up two boxes of Kleenex tissues, trying in vain to stem the flow of mucus from her sinuses whilst I had suffered from sunburn, blissfully dozing, as I had, on an airbed in the motel's pool. Eren's continued absence was causing concern, but later in the day, he rolled back into town having feasted from the menu of the 'Chicken Shack', one of Nevada's numerous licensed brothels.

The unforeseen delay meant we were behind schedule, and after a torturous winding journey during which our navigator, Colette, contrived to lose our way more than once, we finally arrived in Santa Fe thirty minutes before Eren was due on the decks. What Johnny had neglected to mention in advance was that the club night was a hardcore lesbian affair. Not at all a problem other than that the bouncer was the same bull-dyke that had taken potshots at us two years previous. Unrecognized, I slipped through the entrance, but not before being bear-hugged and embraced by the now-friendly bouncer. A matter made worse by the fact that she had neglected to shave that day.

Eren's Las Vegas exertions had left him exhausted and indisposed to make the arduous drive from New Mexico to Los Angeles. I left him in the safe hands of Karen, Johnny's long-suffering girlfriend, instructing her to ensure Eren made it on a later flight from Albuquerque to California and to meet us at the Roosevelt Hotel on Hollywood Boulevard. Johnny filled the vacant seat in the car, and with the rising sun flooding the rear-view mirror, we headed back west across the desert.

The original Los Angeles downtown Art Deco 'Mayan Theater,' built in 1927, had survived as a performance theatre, cinema, adult film house and more recently as a nightclub and music venue. The latest incarnation was in 2022 when the French electronic duo Daft Punk streamed a video recording from their groundbreaking 1997 tour Daftendirektour. Although the authenticity of the building's fabulous exterior and interior bas-relief Mayan facades. Originally constructed in grey concrete, which had been diluted in the 1960s by the addition of bright colours, the building still to this day remains one of the city's architectural jewels. In 1990 it was the only LA venue where House music was regularly featured. Unfortunately, as a showcase for Eren's talent the gig turned out to be a damp squib. Scheduled to play the closing set his predecessor refused to give up the decks and console and by the time the security guards prised him from the turntables the venue was half empty. At the end of the night, members of the Manchester band 'New Order' gave Eren a rapturous applause, and we left to join them for a tequila session on Santa Monica beach. Needing a change of scenery and social behaviour, Colette and I left the others to fend for themselves and drove south across the border into Mexico. This was an era when all that was required to negotiate a border crossing was simply a California driving license. We pulled into Rosarito Beach, a quiet lazy town blighted only by the unsightly waterside location of an oil refinery. Difficult, at the time, to imagine that this location was to be transformed when the film director, James Cameron, re-sank the 'Titanic' in its harbour.

IGNITION

Etched into The Babe's newly-acquired facial tan, the scars of his lengthy incarceration were plain to see. He was only in his early forties but his lined, wrinkled facial features, balding pate and tinged whiteness at the temples had added twenty years to his appearance. His once-piercing cerulean blue eyes were washed out and grey. Within, he had become a man full of hatred and resentment for the system that had propelled him headlong into the horrors of the American Federal penal nightmare. He was vengeful, a man on a crusade whose mission was one of retribution. His intended weapon of mass destruction was LSD. This philosophy clashed dramatically with both Ted and me. Inactivity in the marketplace meant that our supply chains had vanished, and new clients would have to be sought out.

The overall volume of illicit acid had diminished considerably in the USA since the halcyon days twenty years earlier. However, the insatiable demand had remained intact. Whenever it became available there was a baying collection of willing customers. I had brought The Babe up to date on the developing rave culture and the emergence of ecstasy as the prime drug of choice, but I remained firmly convinced that given the socio-economic downturn, LSD would be in a prime position for a revival. Both Ted and I remained privately dismissive of The Babe's maniacal grandiose objectives but with our own egos to satisfy, mine as an artist and Ted's as a chemist, we never voiced our true opinions.

Since my relocation back to California, my relationship with the bartender, Lindy, had blossomed, and we had moved into an apartment together. To supplement her income, she ran the office for a small independent art production company, 'Wet Paint Studios.' Owned and operated by the likeable George Mead, the business specializes in large-format airbrush murals, reproductions for convention displays and stage sets for rock and roll bands. His major and most enduring client was the retail music superstore 'Tower Records' This was the zenith of the era of 12" vinyl records. From its humble inception in Sacramento, California, in 1967, 'Tower' opened the world's largest record store in San Francisco at the corners of Columbus Avenue and Bay Street. A unique feature of the store was the six-foot square reproduction of popular album covers that adorned the building's exterior. Beautifully and exquisitely airbrushed by George's skilled team of professional artists, the paintings would constantly be updated and replaced as new releases hit the market. The quality of the artwork was such that no one ever graffitied the paintings, although there were several attempts to steal the boards from the walls.

In addition to our fine art backgrounds George and I shared a more than passing interest in paper. Mine as a design of blotter and his as a direct descendent of the founder of the Mead Paper Company, who to this day continue to supply to the Federal Bureau of Engraving and Printing the paper on which all United States banknotes are printed. Simply put, his family was in the business of making money! I had enticed George to the Pleasuredome for the *'House Nation'* night, and seeing the potential for a growing club culture, we joined in a project to design and produce two massive murals for a soon-to-open nightclub. *'Big Heart City'* was to use several ultra-violet lighting rigs, so our proposal was to produce a 50-foot and 30-foot-long black light mural, each of which would extend along the club's downstairs sidewalls. Working with black light paint was a trip as under normal daylight or tungsten lighting, the pigments and hues bore no resemblance to their appearance under ultra-violet. To avoid eye strain, we had to mix the colours under UV and paint the murals under normal lighting conditions. The resulting colours' appearance often defied logic and we constantly had to switch the ultra-violet back on to reassure ourselves that the colour mixing was exact. Curiously, my artwork was going from one extreme to another, producing as I was, designs on quarter-inch squares of paper or four-hundred square-foot murals!

The Babe's attempted one-man LSD barrage of the United States was turning out to be nothing more than a delusional pipe dream. He seemed trapped in a time warp under the illusion that a whole new generation of college kids was just itching to get their hands on his precious cargo of LSD. It was the earlier-mentioned external growing economic developments that were to transform my blotter and his production beyond expectations.

In November 1990, a combination of business and pleasure took George and me to London for the weekend. The business was in discussion with Tower Records Piccadilly store over a proposal to paint a series of murals. The pleasure was a 'House' party organized by Neville at a National Heritage Elizabethan house and barn, located in the middle of the Suffolk countryside. Ted had wished us on our way with an ounce bag of freshly synthesized MDA. (The difference between MDA and MDMA is sometimes hard to detect, but I consider MDA to be more psychedelic than MDMA. In The United States, they are colloquially referred to as 'Sally' and 'Molly'). Due to the economic recession that had descended on the UK, the 100 or so guests seemed devoid of the usual rave party favours, so I set about liberally distributing the MDA. The economic malaise was to worsen, but for LSD, a dramatic 'Phoenix from the ashes' awakening was about to materialize. Many youngsters decided to escape the doom and gloom and continue their partying ways in warmer climes. Goa in India became inundated with Western raves, and parties sprung up in Thailand and Indonesia. Others were transporting rave culture further afield to Australia and South Africa, and a few DJs and cult followers had moved to the San Francisco Bay Area. One such group, which hails from Cambridge in the UK, joined with local promoters staging, under the banner of '*ToonTown*', regular legal events as well as impromptu underground parties. Not all of their productions were strictly commercial undertakings. The monthly free 'Full Moon' parties, considered by many to be the best Bay area raves, ran after dark on San Francisco's Baker Beach. Although open to the public, geographically lying as it did within the confines of the Presidio United States Army base, the stretch of sand with its picture-postcard view of the Golden Gate Bridge fell under the administration of the US Federal Government. The San Francisco Police Department had begun to flex its muscles in dealing with illegal parties but was powerless to stop the full moon events as its jurisdiction ended at the gates to the Presidio. The military police who patrolled the area were severely undermanned at night and simply turned a blind eye to the events. Had they been made aware that the couple of hundred kids dancing on the beach were under the influence of LSD and ecstasy, then as the party was taking place in a Federal facility, the FBI or DEA could have been called in to deal with the 'situation.' On one occasion, a military policeman ventured to investigate from the safety of his vehicle onto the beach. He was greeted warmly and handed a joint of marijuana which he gladly accepted. He took a couple of deep tokes, grinned and drifted blissfully back to his car.

Quality ecstasy was soon to be in short supply. More and more partygoers were turning to LSD as their drug of choice to sustain themselves through all-night raves. Welshman Paul Williams and his partner from Birmingham, Michael, ran a regular event in a cavernous warehouse in the East Bay city of Oakland during which they distributed free tabs of acid to all in attendance. The original source of their supply was easy to determine as I immediately recognized my blotter design. Steven Garvey and I had previously known one another from his DJing at 'The Wag' in London's Soho district. He had also briefly dated my sister. Having joined the exodus from the UK, he was now based in Miami, Florida, but was making regular trips to the West Coast to procure and replenish stocks of LSD from Williams. His catchment areas were the University of Miami, Florida and the campus of Florida State in Jacksonville.

Alan, one of the newly arrived Cambridge crowd, had narrowly avoided arrest in England before fleeing to California. His involvement in the 'Batman & Joker' distribution put him under surveillance from the British police but he managed to slip through the police dragnet that had trapped his fellow conspirators. His father, a serving police officer, inadvertently told his son of the impending police swoop and Alan quietly slipped unscathed out of the country. Seems that old habits die hard, as he was now back in the acid business, providing a monthly supply of blotters to the North Carolina student community. Even Michael from Birmingham had posted a few sheets of blotter to friends back home, but tragically, one of his packages was intercepted and the recipient arrested. The amount was relatively small but the overall demand from the United Kingdom for product was increasing dramatically.

I had met all of these suppliers socially but none of them had any idea of my indirect involvement in their dealings. I also knew the intermediaries who passed the LSD on to them and the chemist responsible for the drug's manufacture. I suppose I briefly held a perverse sense of smugness knowing that their enterprises were partly dependent on me. I could easily acquire hundreds of thousands of doses of LSD, but ironically, if ever I wanted a hit or two, I would probably have to search for a street dealer in the city's Haight district. The major concern was that of anonymity and security. As long as The Babe, Ted and myself maintained our collective vow of silence, there was no way we could be connected to one another.

Lindy's fiftieth birthday was looming, exacerbating a mid-life crisis. With bartending and George's office duties her only source of income, she was growing more and more depressed over her long-term security. This concern and unease were having an adverse effect on her overall health. Her bartending co-worker Larry was planning on opening his own drinking establishment but, in need of additional finances, offered Lindy and me a partnership. The '*Fickle Fox*' on Valencia Street in the heart of the Mission District had been a popular neighbourhood bar and restaurant in the 1970s. At the end of the decade, its two owners tragically succumbed to the horror of Aids; the business was foreclosed and put up for sale. Over the following ten years, ownership changed hands numerous times, and when I arrived to view the premises, it was operating as a punk biker bar. The windowless elongated interior was divided into three narrow segments. The bar occupied the front section, a gloomy lounge, and the centre and the back room functioned as a dance floor. The fully-equipped commercial kitchen was still sublet to a catering company, but overall, the property had great potential. Within a week the owner had accepted our offer.

Larry's choice for a name was 'Zanzibar, which was a remarkable coincidence considering that my brother-in-law Sean was now managing a drinking club of the same name in Covent Garden, London and the most famous House music venue in New Jersey, which was also named the 'Zanzibar'. I soon discovered that Larry had very little business acumen or no preconceptions about how to run and operate a bar. His vision was a watering hole where friends could gather and drink into the early hours. Having witnessed his over-generosity whilst serving drinks, any revenue under his supervision would be minimal to say the least. Use of the facility had to be maximized so I outlined a proposal to reopen the kitchen, initially serving tapas during the early evenings and to operate the back room as a dance venue after 10 p.m.

Mexican terracotta tiled flooring was laid, the back bar was painted turquoise and cherry red and kitsch Formica-topped yellow bar tables were installed. Larry's girlfriend Phoebe, a practicing Pop artist, hung a selection of her paintings and a destitute Russian painted a luminescent Keith-Haring style mural on the back wall of the dance room. With a professional DJ console and sound system in place, the quirky, funky-looking 'Zanzibar' opened for business.

It would be another month before the bar began serving food. I had known Carlito, a native Colombian, from my restaurant connections back in the late 1970s. Having trained in France under the Michelin three-star chef Francois Bise, Carlito's culinary skills were beyond reproach, and I was excited when he agreed to run the kitchen at the 'Zanzibar.' Drawing on his Latin and Hispanic roots his unique style of tapas soon had diners flocking to our Mission District eatery. A glowing review from the 'San Francisco Chronicle's' restaurant critic was to firmly establish Carlito's reputation once and for all.

The rapid success of Zanzibar's food operation meant I could now devote my time to the music aspect of the business. I hired local up-and-coming house DJs to play from Thursday evenings through Saturday nights, but most ravers were focused on larger events. Under California's licensing laws and regulations bars and drinking establishments can serve alcohol between the hours of 6 a.m. and 2 a.m. the following morning. Aware that on Saturday nights partygoers are always eager to carry on after clubs close, usually around 6 a.m. I began running after-hours parties at the 'Zanzibar', commencing at six. Each week, by seven o'clock the place was jammed-pack with two hundred revellers dancing to the bass-heavy beat of House music. With its tight intimate surroundings, the bar had a genuine party atmosphere, and the drink receipts surpassed the gross for the remainder of the week. For what, under 'normal' circumstances was a 'dead' time in the bar business, Sunday mornings proved a remarkable success. The Mission District police precinct located two blocks from the Zanzibar was soon made aware of the unusual gatherings, but with patrons always well-behaved and trouble-free, the SFPD paid little attention to our activities. A Honduran illegal alien and his wife had the misfortune to live above the premises, but his status made it impossible to register a formal complaint. I compensated the couple by providing them with complimentary meals in the bar two nights a week.

Luke Simmonds, the landlord of one of the Zanzibar's part-time bartenders, had, over the years gained a reputation as an insatiable collector of LSD blotter art. His house, located two blocks from the bar, was a living attestation with every interior wall covered in samples of blotter art. Small exhibitions of his collection had been staged in the city but in January 1988 the profiles of blotter art and injudiciously Luke himself, who I have always referred to as the 'Curator,' were to be raised, with a show at the appropriately named

Psychedelic Solution Gallery in New York. Reviewed by a New York Times art critic, who remained undecided whether or not the work displayed could be considered art, the show was to arouse enormous interest amongst the general public, bringing to their attention, above ground for the first time, the artwork of an anonymous and unknown group of artists. One evening I was invited into Luke's home. I was shown into the high-ceilinged living room where the Curator's girlfriend was entertaining guests with a piano recital. Her playing sounded discordant and jumbled and when I glanced across at the sheet music from which I assumed she was reading, I saw that the pages were upside down. Mark was holding court in a side room, discussing his blotter collection with a trio of captivated listeners. The cast of characters, ambience and retro decor gave the impression of having stepped back in a time warp to the 1960s.

Expat ravers would congregate nightly at the '*Mad Dog in the Fog*' an English-owned pub. In all my years spent in California, I had shunned the expat community. I hadn't relocated to the West Coast to socialize with the English, read red-topped tabloid newspapers or drink warm beer, but occasionally, I would be out and about promoting the 'Zanzibar's' events.

Donny, originally from Oldham, was down on his luck and cut a lonely and forlorn figure. One evening, I invited him back to the 'Zanzibar' and gave him some work as a bar-back and temporary sleeping quarters in the basement. He stayed a couple of weeks then moved on. A month later, he turned up at the bar with three English acquaintances in tow. They were looking to set up a regular supply line for substantial amounts of LSD and Donny, oblivious to my connections, had suggested that I might be able to steer them in the right direction. One's suspicion is naturally aroused when three strangers come knocking. Their story that they had been living in Los Angeles checked out as they were familiar with the expat haunts, and they also held valid California Driving licenses. Two of them were planning on returning to England within a few days and were anxious to acquire a couple of hundred sample hits of LSD before their departure. The Babe was away in South America renewing his social and business relationship with Carlos and would not return for another ten days. As for Ted, he may have, over time, been responsible for the manufacture of millions of doses, but he rarely partook of the drug and wisely never had anything in his possession. Fate was to intervene from an unexpected source.

Wild Bill was a small-time neighbourhood pot dealer who would constantly boast of his heroic exploits as a Green Beret during the Vietnam War. He had a forward and aggressive demeanour, but the truth was that his flat feet and short-sightedness prevented him from ever being called upon to serve in the military, and his bark was bigger than his bite. In recent years, his health had declined, and to counteract his constant rheumatism, he had started 'chasing the dragon', leading to an uncontrollable heroin habit. His daily routine would bring him lunchtime to the 'Zanzibar' to hang out with Larry, the two taking it, in turn, to smoke 'Mexican Brown' heroin in the basement. When I arrived, Larry was already nodding off behind the bar. Not a good advertisement for the daytime business! I walked into the basement office just as Wild Bill was laying out a fresh piece of tinfoil for another pipe. Knowing of my disapproval of heroin, he was suddenly taken aback, and a look of guilt spread across his face. He was like a kid who had just been caught with his hand in the cookie jar.

In an attempted appeasement he raised the subject of LSD. According to Bill, he had a few hundred hits of 'primo acid' which had apparently been:

"Made available from Timothy Leary's private stash!"

His suggestion was that some of my rave connections might be interested in the acid.

An interesting sales pitch, but the fact that he had some products couldn't have come at a better time. He took out from a shoulder bag a block of two hundred blotters decorated with what he called:

'*Knights Templar Shields.*' I was staring at a half sheet of my most recent design. It was a scary thought imagining Wild Bill on acid, but 'God' certainly does move in mysterious ways. I paid Bill for his entire stash, giving him enough cash to keep him in 'brown' for the rest of the week. The following evening the two Englishmen arrived and collected the samples. The third member of the group was to remain in Los Angeles, and in the future, he would liaise with me directly.

The Babe returned from Brazil flushed with success. 200,000 doses of the newly designed 'Heraldic Shield' blotter would soon be on their way to South America. I mentioned my meeting with the potential new clients; however, his reaction was less sanguine than I had hoped. There was no question he could handle any eventuality, but fulfilling Carlos' order would require all of my remaining stock of blotter paper. With a backlog of work at the printers, it would be two weeks before I had additional supplies to hand.

The call came from Los Angeles with an initial order for 50,000 to be collected in ten days. The fresh 'Shield' blotter was a week away from completion, but the LA connection was flying up to San Francisco in two days and also urgently needed his precious collection and set about dipping the five thousand hits. The Los Angeles contact and his partners were obviously new to the LSD scene, intent as they were on simply parcelling the impregnated blotter and shipping it directly via the United States Parcel Service to the UK. I pointed out that without some basic precautions, 5000 hits. I persuaded the 'Curator' to part with five sheets of *'Lotus'* blotter from

there was always the possibility that customs officials could intercept and identify their contraband. Simply wrapping a consignment in carbon paper would at least eliminate detection by way of X-ray. As each individual package would be at least an inch thick, I suggested that they acquire and use A4-sized custom packets from different Los Angeles bookshops. Under any preliminary examination, this would indicate that the contents were merely a book from a California retailer to a customer in the UK. For future parcels, the bookstore and postal location could be varied and changed.

The Englishmen had requested that all their purchases, for the sake of continuity, be impregnated onto paper with a blotter design that was produced solely for their target market. When he turned up to collect the first order of 50,000 hits, he was surprised to see the '*Shield*' design rather than the 'Lotus.' From then on and for the next three months he collected weekly supplies of the shield design with the only variation being a change of background colour. In the space of the next few months 800.000 doses of 'shield' LSD crossed the Atlantic. At that time, I had difficulty imagining such huge quantities being regularly consumed in the UK. It was not until thirty years later that I was to discover the final destinations of those orders.

The Babe's general psychological well-being was giving Ted and me increasing cause for concern. Since his release from prison, he had been on an extended course of treatment and medication for depression. His persistent megalomaniacal grandiose plans were becoming obsessive and his behaviour irrational. We both believed he was in an advanced state of psychosis, amplified by his addiction to prescription drugs. It came as no surprise to hear that after twenty years of friendship and cooperation, Ted finally severed all connection with his friend. The Babes' scathing comments were the final straw for me, and the following day I changed my phone number.

It was apparent that Ted had been giving serious thought to parting company and unbeknown to The Babe had already entered into a business arrangement with another Bay Area aficionado. Without having to meet or know anyone but Ted, I agreed to continue to design and produce blotter. The first account was to be the ongoing business with the Englishmen whose insatiable thirst for acid remained unquenched. Their demand became irksome as someone overseas had counterfeited the 'shield' design and was selling unimpregnated blotter. Each month I had to change the design.

A conversation with the 'curator' revealed a hitherto unknown piece of trade gossip. According to Luke, it was rumoured that in an effort to curtail the production of blotter, the United States Federal Government had imposed licensing restrictions on the commercial use of perforation machinery. The story was that companies and print operations were to be strictly vetted and inspected by government officials. This piece of gossip seemed highly implausible, and besides, if it were true, then somebody had neglected to mention this significant development to my printer.

The indirect consequences were that I suddenly found myself to be the sole producer of printed and perforated blotter paper in the Western United States! It wasn't long before unsolicited requests flooded in for my services. One individual wanted an Irish Republican logo incorporated into a blotter design. Although somewhat sympathetic to the Republican cause, I could never condone the modus operandi of the militant elements of the IRA, and political statements on blotter were strictly verboten. Incomprehensibly, the same person contacted me the following week requesting the red hand logo of the Ulster Loyalists as an alternative! I suppose Harold Wilson's statement that "A week in politics is a long time." couldn't be truer.

The more extensive and widespread my work became, the greater the interest shown by the Federal authorities. Under the United States legal system, the production of blotter wasn't exactly a crime, but my anonymity was no longer a reality. I had sanctioned Ted to initiate more and more connections, and consequentially, within me, a feeling of unease arose. I sensed that storm clouds were gathering. From the obvious distress in the girlfriend's voice, I sensed immediately that the 'Curator' was in trouble. She had telephoned to tell me that Mark was in custody somewhere in Oakland. I drove straight to their house, removing a small amount of marijuana, three caps of ecstasy and half a dozen tabs of acid. It was not exactly a major drug haul, but at least the premises were now 'clean.' Luke, in the hands of the Feds, was to be transferred to Houston, Texas, to face the unlikely and laughable charge of trafficking. To suggest that the art collector was a major player was ludicrous and the charges had to be trumped up. However, he may know someone who would be invaluable to the authorities. The case collapsed before it started as the only evidence was a witness statement from a small-time dealer who had already negotiated a plea bargain with the local District Attorney. As an unreliable witness, his statement was ruled inadmissible by the judge, and Luke was on his way home.

The United States Drug Enforcement Agency (DEA) had set up a special regional LSD task force in the San Francisco Federal Building located at 450 Golden Gate Avenue, close to the Civic Center. Under the auspices of Agent Arty Hubbard, the unit had been assigned to douse 'the keepers of the flame' of the underground LSD manufacture and supply that had burned unabated since the late 1960s. The 'Curator' continued to exhibit artwork and to voice his disdain for the authorities, but following his brush with the Feds, his heightened profile unnerved many of the players, and some left Northern California on extended vacations.

I had chosen to take a back seat from the Zanzibar, venturing occasionally only to dine on Carlito's cuisine. Unbeknownst to me, Larry and Lindy had signed over the food concession indefinitely to the wily Colombian. With Larry drifting deeper into heroin addiction, Lindy couldn't cope with the additional responsibilities, and her day-to-day involvement diminished, leaving Carlito with a virtual carte blanche.

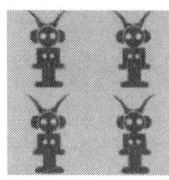

GEISERVILLE

Given the perceived increasing threat of possible exposure in the Bay Area, I needed to get out of the city until I felt safe enough to return. I headed to New York City to spend some time with an old friend, David Geiser. We had first met fifteen years earlier in San Francisco, where David, an emigre from Rochester, New York, had worked as an illustrator producing drawings for a series of underground comics. He had found his work as a commercial artist unfulfilling and turned his attention to Fine Art. His abstract expressionist painting became a full-time occupation, and only a monthly visit to San Francisco by a mutual friend, the Gonzo journalist Hunter S Thompson, would drag David temporarily away from his canvases. Under the auspices of the San Francisco Examiner's feature editor, Warren Hinkle, Thompson had been offered a regular column in the newspaper. Hunter would visit the city from his home outside Aspen, Colorado, ostensibly to cash his checks from the newspaper, but he had a long-standing friendship with Warren. Not that they needed an excuse to party! Geiser had known Hinkle from his magazine days, so when Hunter arrived in town, Warren would call David, and David would phone me. To call our encounters drinking gatherings would be something of an understatement. The session always began at the same location, a neighbourhood Irish bar off of 17th. Street. My first visit to the drinking establishment had almost been inauspicious. The owners, Irish immigrants, were die-hard Republicans, and before your lips touched the rim of the first glass of Guinness, a collection tray was passed around 'For the Cause' I dreaded the thought that they would become aware of my British nationality, but introduced as Kevin It was naturally assumed I had Irish ancestry. Having read

Hunter's epic 1971 account "Fear and Loathing" I was curious to know more of the 'sheets of blotter' found in the opening chapter that formed part of the cornucopia of drugs in the trunk of the red Chevy convertible on Hunter and his attorney's drive to Las Vegas.

On questioning him regarding the blotter's imagery, Hunter initially stared at me quizzically and then a wry smile spread across his face.

"Now I think about it. It was a 'windowpane'. Not blotter!"

'Windowpane' was a popular alternative form of LSD distribution consisting of translucent plain sheets of gelatine squares. I felt deflated. I had hoped that one of the early classic blotter images, such as Mickey Mouse's 'Sorcerer's Apprentice, ' might have adorned the blotter. Of course, the whole thing could have been fictitious and merely a literary effect to enhance the narrative.

After a few pints and shots of Bushmills whisky, the binge continued in the bohemian North Beach district. I can't imagine what passers-by thought of our boisterous quartet. Hunter with his yellow-tinted shades perpetually smoking his Dunhills through a cigarette holder. Whilst Hinkle with his black eye patch looking every part a swashbuckler, never went anywhere without his Basset hound 'Bentley' in tow. Geiser bespattered in paint, trying to look every bit like a reincarnation of Jackson Pollack and I, with my shoulder-length hair and snakeskin boots, passing myself off as some mysterious rock musician. After a day or so, Geiser and I would succumb to 'impaired decision making', but the relentless duo of Thompson and Hinkle would continue off into the sunset.

Geiser's paintings were beginning to show promise, but New York, the centre of the art world, was where the action was, so David moved back East. In the ensuing years, through a combination of hard work and shrewd networking, he had prospered from the philanthropic support of a core group of devoted followers and had set up his studio in a 3000 square foot space on Lower Broadway in Manhattan. His patrons fell into two distinct categories. Either

Uptown socialites or characters from New York's collection of bizarre underworld misfits.

An uneventful evening at McSorley's Old Ale House, A New York Irish institution, was ending. As we ambled from the watering hole back towards the studio Geiser suddenly remembered we were close to an art patron whose account was long overdue. One morning hardly seemed an appropriate time for a debt collection but I was assured that Wolf never slept. Besides, if no funds were available at least I would be on hand to assist in the removal of an artwork from the wall. When the long black-haired goth, caked in black eye makeup and dressed in a body-hugging black leather catsuit, opened the door, it didn't feel like we were about to enter the normal run-of-the-mill classic middle-class American scene of domestic bliss. At the end of a long, narrow, dark-painted hallway dimly lit by flickering wall candles, we were shown into the 'Master's' bedroom. Seated bolt upright in bed and dressed in a shabby pair of striped pyjamas was a grey-haired Rasputin-like figure with piercing Charles Manson eyes. A sense of trepidation made me want to apologize for the late-night intrusion, but anticipating my thought, Geiser assured me that Wolf only ever got out of bed to visit the bathroom. To the right of the bed stood an ornate hardwood mediaeval throne with a studded red leather seat, on which rested a black telephone. To the left of the bedroom doorway, mounted on a stand, was a Sony colour VCR monitor showing a film of a group of individuals clad in Nazi SS uniforms and engaged in the crucifixion of a compliant victim. The only other item of furniture in the room was an ornate birdcage in which a sleeping macaw was perched. Wolf proffered a lame excuse of why he was unable to pay his debt to Geiser, pausing occasionally when attended by one of the three dominatrices who were off duty from the famous Westside Sadomasochism (S&M) venue that he owned and operated.

Thankfully, Wolf's imaginative monologue was brought to an abrupt end when the macaw awoke and uttered a shrill obscenity. Enraged by the interruption, the torture chamber's proprietor drew from under the bedclothes a 357-magnum handgun discharging a round into the ceiling. Glancing upward I noticed the other pot marks on the plasterwork. Undoubtedly the consequences of prior disagreements with his feathered companion. Whatever the truth surrounding Wolf's financial circumstances I thought the hour was inopportune to try to remove a painting from the house. The following day lacked the drama and colour of the previous night, but Geiser did at least procure a commission from the daughter of the owner of a leading gallery.

Tucked away off of Canal Street in Greenwich Village, *'Liquid Sky'* was one of New York's first stores to specialize in marketing products that reflected the city's developing English-style club culture. I was introduced to the Portuguese-speaking owner by Richard Henderson, an ex-Bay Area rave organizer. He proudly displayed in the store a poster from the 'Curator's' 1988 'Cure of Souls' New York blotter art exhibition. Having previously failed in his attempts to obtain any samples of blotter artwork he was delighted at the prospect of finally acquiring some sheets when next I visited New York. What he was totally unprepared for was the surprise revelation that, in the interim, I had incorporated Liquid Sky's logo, a pre-Columbian extra-terrestrial figurine, into a blotter design.

I had barely been away for a week, but the demand for blotters, both dipped and undipped, had remained unabated. I retrieved several 'urgent' messages from my answering service. A DJ from Goa, an English woman living in Tokyo, a student from South Carolina, and even a fellow graphic designer's college buddy from Florida were in town kicking their heels and anxiously awaiting my return.

One of the LA English connections showed up unexpectedly, looking for me at the 'Zanzibar.' He explained that he had had to temporarily shut down his UK operation when two deliveries from California had failed to arrive at their destination. I pointed out the obvious danger of sending impregnated paper across transcontinental routes and advised him to minimize the risk by separating the transportation of the paper from the liquid or powder form of LSD. He asked to meet the 'Curator' socially, so the next day, we stopped off at Luke's house. The Englishman seemed curious to understand the dipping process which the Curator was only too willing to outline to him. I would have personally provided him with a demonstration, but inexplicably, he must have assumed that my sole responsibility was simply the design and paper production. This relatively innocuous meeting was to personally have a far greater significance in the events that were to transpire the following year.

Concern for Michael from Birmingham's well-being and deteriorating mental health had led to his friend Paul O'Neil pleading for my intervention. In repeated attempts to fulfill a death wish Micheal had taken to driving his BMW at night and at break-neck speed with the car's headlights switched off. After much persuasion, he agreed to join me on a trip to Santa Fe for a reunion with my old friend Johnny. Michael had promised to stay drug-free during our short break in New Mexico, but whilst fumbling through his hold-all on our flight to Albuquerque, he stumbled across an ounce bag of 'missing' MDMA powder. At the car rental desk, we treated ourselves to an oversized new model Cadillac, engaged the vehicle's cruise control and headed north to Santa Fe. I'd planned to hook up with Johnny at the end of the short break, so we headed towards Taos. After a relaxing couple of days, we headed back towards Santa Fe. Following a hair-raising fifty-mile drive through Chaco Canyon, during which we did our best to wreck the Cadillac's suspension, we pulled up outside Johnny and Karen's ranch house. A welcome Southwestern meal of tortillas and chilli Verde awaited us, and as a reward for our generous host's hospitality, Michael passed around his bag of MDMA. It had been three days since he'd gone on the wagon, so a little powder was unlikely to push him over the edge. In the company of good friends, we sat outside, chatted and stared at the starlit sky as a full moon rose over the high mesa.

It had been a relaxing and rejuvenating time, but the stress we had gone out of our way to avoid resurfaced on the return drive to Albuquerque. The ease and comfort of driving the Cadillac had led me to assume that we were travelling at a slower speed than was the case. That at least was the feeble excuse I offered when we were pulled over by a state trooper for travelling at 42 mph in a thirty zone. At first, I thought the officer had made a mistake as we were travelling on an open highway with only the adjacent New Mexico State penitentiary as the only sign of civilization for miles. Unfortunately, and unbeknown to me, there was a speed restriction imposed on all traffic in the immediate vicinity of a state prison. If there had been a warning sign, then I would have missed it completely. Not satisfied with just issuing a speeding ticket, the Native American officer from the Navajo Reservation Police Department requested to see Michael's and my driving licenses and the vehicle's registration. I handed over my Californian and Michael's British driving license, but as Michael opened the glove compartment to remove the registration documents, a pile of crumpled dollar bills cascaded to the floor from a brown paper bag. On our drive throughout the state, Michael insisted on paying for the petrol in cash each time we had to refill the Caddy's gas-guzzling tank. Having stuffed the change into the brown bag, the net result was that we had accumulated an unusually large number of dollar bills. All the police officer could see was a pile of cash, and from his viewpoint, they could have been hundred-dollar bills. Not only that, but the rental had Idaho plates. With two speeding Englishmen, a stash of cash and a brand-new Cadillac with out-of-state license plates, his suspicions were aroused.

"Excuse me, sir, would you mind stepping out of the vehicle and opening the trunk?"

Michael's ashen face gave himself away. I knew at once that the MDMA powder was in the trunk. I may not have been aware of the speeding restrictions in place, but I did know that only a Highway Patrol officer or County Sheriff had the authority to search the car.

"I have no objection to you looking inside the trunk officer. We will be waiting right here for you when you get back with a search warrant!"

The next few seconds seemed like an eternity until a forced smile etched from the policeman's mouth.

"Just remember Mr. Barron. Next time you may not be so lucky."

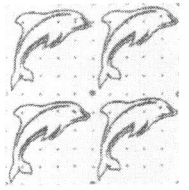

GATHERING STORM CLOUDS

The narrow escape in New Mexico and the cop's departing words echoed in my mind and finally reinforced a decision that I had been struggling to make for months but one I could no longer postpone. I would close the blotter business at the end of the year. Over lunch at the Zuni Cafe, I informed Ted of my reasons and the conclusions I had reached. Since The Babe's release from prison, the only motivational force that had kept me in production was a combination of artistic ego and, to a limited extent, the financial rewards. Any relevance, meaning and the occasional sense of humour had been superseded in recent times by a collection of mainly superficial, fatuous and hackneyed marketing images. I had just as well been designing candy bar wrappers.

In the United States until the late 1980s, the LSD industry was generally a close-knit group of devoted and dedicated individuals who had never been guided by the profit motive, but with the drug's rebirth in the early 1990s, insalubrious characters were emerging. Links with people of dubious distinction had drawn attention to long-standing members of the community and it would be a matter of time before someone put our names in the frame. Enclosed as I had become by a strange almost intuitive sense of impending danger, I decided to take a 'sabbatical' and leave the United States for an indeterminate period of time. I voiced my intention to my co-partners at the Zanzibar, effectively giving up any further involvement in the bar enterprise. It was just a few days before my last Christmas in America. For the second time in recent weeks, I was unexpectedly revisited by the Englishman from the LA connection. In a period of under two years, over two million hits of acid had passed through the hands of the UK-based troika. It turned out that the trio had now gone their separate ways and the individual standing before me was seeking technical assistance regarding the production of blotter back in England. I had repeatedly advised him and his partners on the prudence of avoiding transatlantic shipping methods, but my counsel had gone unheeded, and consignments had gone missing. Despite a generous financial consultation fee, my decision to retire was final and irreversible. Before departing, the Englishman left me his British phone number insisting that I should call him as I had mentioned that London would be my first port of call after leaving the States. He wanted, for old times' sake, to express his gratitude by taking me out for dinner.

My graphics assistant was in such a state that it took a little time to extricate the complete story. His former college buddy, to whom I had passed 2000 hits of acid, had been arrested in his hometown of Panama City, Florida. Less than twenty-four hours later, I received more bad news from Ted. A local Northern Californian father and son duo, recipients of several sheets of freshly designed and dipped FBI logo blotter, had been taken into custody.

I dropped off a batch of purple and gold 'Shield' blotter at the Curator's house for his collection and the L.A. Englishman flew up to collect my remaining paper stock. When he handed me the manila envelope containing several thousand hundred dollar bills, I noticed that a United States Treasury Department paper seal had been attached to the previously opened envelope, and the addressee was none other than my recent visitor from the UK, who apparently still maintained a residence in Santa Monica. The two of them were no longer in business, so what was he doing with an envelope of cash addressed to his former partner? There were fifteen thousand dollars. I was exacerbated by their naivete and crass stupidity. Had they not realized they were in contravention of Federal currency restrictions. The bills were probably marked, and the serial numbers were undoubtedly recorded.

I had promised Ted, for my final throw of the dice, that on my way to Europe, I would stop over in New York and, on his behalf, dip one last batch. With the sudden turn of events, the journey east was brought forward in a week. Robby, the Irish courier, carrying thirty grams of crystal dissolved in a litre bottle of Polish vodka and a hold-all containing the blotter paper left from Oakland on a coast-to-coast Amtrak train. His instructions were to deliver in person the paper and liquid to the client and then meet me off my flight from San Francisco at Newark airport, where I would pay him the fee for his services. I decided to alter my travel plans, so instead of flying to London from New York straight after the impregnation work, I intended to fly to Montreal on a one-way ticket where I would then buy a ticket to London.

The courier was at the New Jersey airport concourse, but he still had in his possession the hold-all and, I presumed, the vodka bottle. He had followed Ted's instructions to the tee, having taken a cab from the railroad station to the client's address. The Westside apartment building's concierge had buzzed him into the reception area, where he was notified that he had missed the client by thirty minutes and, more alarmingly, had been led away in handcuffs.

Worryingly, Ted's San Francisco phone number had been disconnected, and two DEA officials had shown up at the Zanzibar enquiring about my whereabouts. I told the courier to dispose of the hold-all containing the paper, took the vodka bottle from him and headed back into Manhattan. The cab driver dropped me off on 2nd Avenue at the British Consulate where I reported a lost passport. It would be twenty-four harrowing hours before I could collect my temporary replacement passport. The wait seemed interminable, but all being well, I would soon be on a flight out of the country. Any sense of relief was tempered until such time as my flight to the UK finally left US airspace.

GOLDEN JUBILEE

My temporary passport was only valid for transit to London and was surrendered to immigration officials at Heathrow. I passed through customs and declared a recently purchased wristwatch as having paid £35.00 in duty. The litre vodka containing dissolved crystal was assumed to be my duty-free purchase. I travelled directly to the passport office in Victoria and filed my application for a new passport. I hadn't been in touch with Cordell for some time. My parents had had difficulty speaking with him, but his mother had effectively barred all their attempts at communication. I made several unsuccessful attempts to contact Julie. It was extremely frustrating, but it wasn't the first time that I had come up against this brick wall.

I tried calling Ted from a phone box but was unable to reach him. His exact circumstances and location worryingly remained unknown. I had Ted's Amsterdam connection details and made contact with his friend, the affable Lennart Dykstra. We had met one another on a previous occasion when the Dutchman had visited California. I explained the ongoing situation and we agreed to meet in Amsterdam once I had been issued with the new travel documents. Lennart collected me from Schiphol airport, and we drove into the city. Along the way, I explained the circumstances and difficulties that had recently unfolded and offered the Dutchman the thirty grams of crystal in my possession. It would take time to offload such a large consignment, but in the meantime, I was facing a minor financial problem. In my haste to flee the States.

I had been unable to retrieve any of my assets and was using an American Express card for my day-to-day expenses. The only practical alternative was to take up the consultation offer extended to me the previous December. I briefed the Englishman's printer on the methodology of paper and perforation production, but within a week, he backed out of the project, and I was asked to help in the search for an alternative. Given my financial problems, it was difficult to refuse the generous offer I received, and besides, I had an ideal substitute printer available

Almost twenty years had passed since I last saw Dean. He had operated a small printing firm in Covent Garden and although I had never required his professional services, we used to meet up once a week for a game of squash. He had always yearned for a more adventurous lifestyle, so it came as no surprise to hear he had sold the printing business, bought a thirty-foot sloop and set off on a solo round-the-world sailing expedition. After a spell in Australia and a brief period of incarceration at the hands of the Israelis, who had suspected him of aiding and abetting Palestinian terrorists, Dean finally returned safely to the UK. Marriage and fatherhood provided the perfect antidote for his wanderlust, and he settled back on the south coast, back in the printing game. I tracked him down offering him a commission to produce three thousand sheets of blotter. The only question remaining was the image to be imprinted, but given the year was 1993, only one theme would warrant serious consideration.

It had been fifty years since LSD's founding father, Albert Hofmann, had accidentally ingested a dose of the drug, first feeling the full effects of his discovery whilst bicycling home from his laboratory. The event in 1943 had been enshrined in LSD's folklore, and for many years, the anniversary had been celebrated by acidheads worldwide. For the Golden Jubilee festivities in England a series of seminars by the renowned psychedelic luminary Alexander Shulgin will culminate on April 16th with a traditional bicycle ride beginning from London's Marble Arch. In many countries, memorable national and international events are marked in diverse ways, but the traditional issue of postal services of commemorative stamps has become commonplace throughout the world. On each A4 sheet of paper the initials 'AH' would be inset into each of the thousand perforated quarter-inch squares. Divided into two columns of five equal rectangles, each containing one hundred squares, the rectangles would be imprinted with a bicycling figure, a profile of Queen Elizabeth's head and the commemorative date. On the reverse side would appear a public health warning:

'DO NOT LICK THESE STAMPS'

In Amsterdam, Lennart had started to shift some of the thirty grams of crystal and an overseas buyer had expressed an interest in purchasing the remaining supply. However, he would be unable to travel to Holland for a further two months. Dean had provided some paper samples for testing, and the Englishman had paid in advance. In addition, he had provided me with an alternative ID, which would be an essential precaution to enable my safe return to the States in the foreseeable future. With time to kill, I turned my attention to more relaxing matters and a holiday somewhere in the sunshine.

The first time I met Eleanor in San Francisco, three years earlier, a brief amorous spark was ignited. We had more recently spent the night together prior to my departure for New York, and coincidentally, she was planning on taking her annual vacation in Europe. I met her off her flight at Brussels airport. Together, we crossed to England, where I was hoping to finalize the Golden Jubilee printing edition. I had intended to make the paper available in time for the fiftieth anniversary, but the plan had to be shelved as Dean had had issues obtaining the right quality paper. With the Englishman's advance, I bought a second-hand Range Rover, and Eleanor and I set off for Southern Europe. Before leaving, I instructed Dean to mail the awaited paper samples to an address in Athens. We drove via Amsterdam and agreed to contact Lennart upon arriving in Greece. When there was a fixed date for his client to fly to Holland, I would make the necessary travel arrangements to return to Amsterdam to make the dip.

Our journey through Luxembourg, Germany and Switzerland passed uneventfully until we crossed into Italy. We pulled into a village on the shores of Lake Comoand, at a local waterside *trattoria*, joined a crowd of Italians who were enjoying a traditional family Sunday lunch. It was an ideal day: a cloudless, sunny sky and the lake's water like a sheet of glass. Having put the recent traumatic events in America behind me, I was beginning to relax for the first time in weeks. After a lunch of grilled fish and two bottles of Orvieto wine, Eleanor and I were now in vacation mode.

Her inspired suggestion that we drop some acid on the drive into Milan seemed like a perfectly good idea at the time. The ride from Como by the autostrada would take less than an hour, so by the time the acid kicked in we should be safely ensconced in a hotel room. What I hadn't considered was the strength of the doses which were part of Ted's 1000-mic 'Private Reserve' This pure batch was ten times stronger than an average street dose and comparable to some of the high doses consumed in the late 1960s. By the time we reached the Piazza Duomo in central Milan, the buildings were beginning to melt.

Along a narrow side street, Eleanor spotted an array of flags of the world fluttering above the entrance to a four-star hotel. I was in no fit state to handle a conversation with the receptionist as my mind had focused on the coloured rivulets flowing down the centre of the road. Eleanor gestured that she had handled the obligatory registration, and together we stepped into the hotel's futuristic stainless-steel elevator. Imagining I was in some intergalactic transportation device, it came as a disappointment when the doors opened on the fifth-floor corridor. 'Reality' returned momentarily when I remembered I had left behind in the car a briefcase containing cash and another fifty hits of Ted's private stash. With Eleanor tantalizingly waving the key to room 528 in front of my eyes the doors to the elevator closed, and I returned to planet reception. The distant thought that I should park the car kept reverberating through my brain. So following the receptionist's instructions that I should turn to the right, I started up the Range Rover's engine. There was no obvious indication of a car park, so I drove fifty metres to the end of the street. I focused briefly on the cross street ahead.

To my left was a fenced area of parkland, and to the right was a row of boutiques but no sign of any car park. I followed the 'Sensa Unico' (one-way street) signpost to the left, then another and another until, eventually the one-way system led me back to the Piazza Duomo. I felt a sense of relief finding myself in somewhat familiar territory, but slowly, the nightmare of my true situation began to dawn. Under the earlier distractions caused by the intensity of the acid, I had completely forgotten the name of the hotel and the street on which it stood! Lost as I had become in the maelstrom of Milan's one-way system.I had no way of finding my way back to Eleanor. I drove onward praying some higher power might intervene on my behalf. Every so often I would be overwhelmed by a wave of intense visual hallucinations and was forced to stop the car. When I eventually spotted a circular street sign with a diagonal black line painted through the word 'Milano' I realized I had driven almost out of the city. Back once again at the 'Piazza Duomo', I stopped to seek assistance from a street hooker whose only words of English were:

"One hundred thousand Lira."

Far from receding, the effects of the acid were getting stronger and after the umpteenth tour of the Piazza, the same hooker, convinced I was a willing punter, began grinning like a Cheshire cat. The sight of her repellent lurid fluorescent lipstick was not having the desired effect. Through my tangled mental confusion, I was struggling to review the facts. All I could recall was a hotel room key number 528 and a hazy vision of four silver stars below a row of flags. I set upon the idea of thumbing through the Milan Yellow Pages under the 'Hotel' section on the off chance a name might light up before my eyes. At a street bar, I ordered a glass of Cynar, an Italian aperitif made from artichokes. The design on the bottle's label looked inviting, but the beverage's disgusting taste resurrected a vivid childhood memory of the family doctor forcing me to swallow some hideous concoction to relieve constipation. I fled to the toilet with a copy of the Yellow Pages. Seated in a locked cubicle, I frantically thumbed through the pages until I reached the letter H. Now, in most countries, the hotel listings are normally found under H, somewhere between G and I. With minimal spoken Italian and hardly any vocabulary, I had no idea that hotels were listed under 'Alberghi.'

"How could the Milanese omit the hotel listings from the yellow pages?"

It had been almost five hours since I told Eleanor I was just returning to the car to fetch the briefcase, and I still had no way of knowing where she was, let alone how she was handling her trip. The effects of the drug had receded sufficiently that I felt I could hold a reasonably normal conversation with another member of the human race. Across the street from the bar was another four-star hotel. Convinced that there couldn't possibly be that many four-star hotels in Milan, I explained to the concierge that I was in town to meet a friend and had forgotten the hotel's name. I was more than surprised to discover that there were at least 80 four-star hotels in the city! I was furnished with a list under 'A' and I began working my way down the page methodically. I now knew how Archimedes felt that day in the bath. A trumpet fanfare echoed in my head as I found my 'Eureka' moment. The word 'Poliziano' popped off the page. Polizia, the Italian word for police! I concluded that somehow, with my problems in America unresolved, my subconscious must have obliterated the word from my mind.

The Poliziano's receptionist was curious to know where I had been the last hours. I explained that I had had difficulty parking the car. She led me outside and, on the wall, immediately to the right of the entrance, she pressed the red button. The slatted metal door rose slowly, revealing the hotel's underground car park. Eleanor's evening had been uneventful as she had spent most of the time in the shower watching the water drain down the plughole. Psychedelic pioneers will often emphasize the principles of 'Set' and 'Setting' before venturing on a psychedelic voyage of discovery. To these edicts, I would add 'Parking the Car.'

The ferry from Ancona took us across the Adriatic, stopping briefly at the island of Corfu before sailing to its destination, the Greek port of Patras. Within three hours, we had arrived in Athens. A Federal Express was awaiting our arrival at the Astir Palace Hotel in Vouliagmeni. From the fifteen examples of the tested paper, I selected two, which I express-mailed back to Dean. An update from Lennart confirmed there would be no movement on the Amsterdam front for a further two weeks. Having decided to remain in Greece for the summer we began searching for suitable accommodation on the island of Crete. A location that I was more than familiar with, stretching back many years. We chanced upon a quiet cloistered, whitewashed house with a shaded waterside terrace. Set far enough from the bustle of the nearest town, the property was an ideal location to while awaythe summer months. To family and friends, we gave a Poste Restante address, and every second day, I would walk a kilometre through an olive grove to use the local taverna's telephone to check on Deans and Lennart's progress. April the 16th arrived, and I felt a tinge of disappointment that the Jubilee blotter wasn't available for release. Nevertheless, to celebrate the occasion Eleanor and I replicated Albert Hofmann's memorable experience by taking a bicycle ride on a less hair-raising 200 mics of Ted's acid. A week later, we were on our way to Amsterdam via Brussels.

I'd expressed to Lennart that my concern for Dean's delays with paper suppliers meant I would be unable to meet his deadline, but he assured me that he had uncovered a batch of local 'Strawberry' paper which would serve the purpose more than adequately. Several hours later we celebrated the completion of the dipping process with a cold beer at the Krasnapolsky Hotel bar. I sat reminiscing of the time I first met Ted at that very bar nearly twenty years ago. Lennart smiled and dialled a number on his mobile phone.

"There is somebody who wants to talk to you."

Ted had ended up in Prague, the capital of the country since renamed Czechia. A whole host of arrests had been made back in California and other associates from as far afield as Louisiana and the Carolinas had been scooped up in a major DEA operation. It turned out that Ted had neglected to pay his phone bill and the utility company had simply disconnected the line. He had only heard about the New York events when Robby, the courier, returned to California. He had packed his bags and used the tried and tested Mexico escape route to flee the country. More worrying was the fate of the LA connection and whether there was still a link to the Englishman. I telephoned to find out if there was any ongoing involvement with LA, but the Englishman assured me that by mutual consent, they had terminated their arrangements a year earlier. The Amsterdam job had been tiring, but Ted, in his generosity, instructed Lennart to pay me a bonus that would cover any financial concerns for the foreseeable future. We headed back to Greece.

The final Jubilee proofs from Dean arrived in the post at the end of June. Prior to their arrival, I had begun to think that the work would never be completed and had seriously considered cancelling the project and returning the Englishman's advance. The offer of a legitimate alternative ID was too tempting and would facilitate my safe return to the US, so I instructed Dean to push forward with the printing. I was naturally concerned with events back in California but I reassured myself that under US Federal law I was unlikely to be arrested for merely producing decorative perforated sheets of paper The summer tourist season on the island of Crete was in full flow, and the peace and tranquility we had cherished earlier in the year had passed. We set off on a convoluted journey back to England detouring through Southern France so that Eleanor could catch up with a friend from back home in California. I mailed from Bordeaux a proof sheet of the 'Jubilee' to the Curator, and we slipped across the Channel into the UK. Back in London, I rented a first-floor Kensington apartment from a friend and, having checked on the progress of the printing, arranged to meet the Englishman in Soho. We rendezvoused at a Dean Street, Soho coffee shop.

Enclosed in an A4 manila envelope, which I concealed inside my jacket, were four sample sheets of the different blotter colour combinations. I asked the Englishman to briefly wait with Eleanor whilst I popped up the street to pay a quick visit to my sister, who, at the time, was having a boyfriend issue. She had found herself in a physically violent relationship but was unable to extricate herself as her partner was unwilling to vacate her apartment. My only advice was that she should consider moving out herself at the earliest possible time. I stayed ten minutes and, on leaving her apartment, was now clasping the manila envelope in my hand. I passed the sealed envelope to the Englishman, who would contact me the following week once his courier had arrived from California with the consignment of liquid LSD. I had enough paper to dip three million doses, but initially, only 100,000 was required. Once the task was complete and in addition to my fee, I was to receive a valid British passport in the name of Christopher Brian Morrison. In the interim, with my new identity now known, I could at least make provisional travel arrangements. The plan was to fly to New York the following Tuesday which would give me the weekend before I could complete the dip. Before leaving, the Englishman handed me an eye dropper containing a small sample amount of LSD that I could test before Saturday. It would be an odd thing to do as why would I need to test the product? It didn't make sense, but in retrospect, it was a key part of a puzzle. All being well, I would have ample time to dip and sanitize the apartment and Eleanor and I could spend the following day, Monday, doing some last-minute shopping.

I was expecting a phone call from the Englishman before the weekend, but when it finally arrived, I was surprised to hear that he was delayed and out of the country. Nevertheless, his courier had landed back in the UK and would be dropping off the acid around mid-afternoon on Saturday. I purchased a litre of methanol, the intended solvent, and we sat back and waited for the delivery. The courier showed up late and disappointingly with no acid available to dip until five o'clock on Sunday. This would mean that we had a tighter schedule if we were to catch Tuesday's New York flight. Before departing, he asked if he could check the paper, so I showed him into the bedroom and opened one of the six cardboard boxes containing the three thousand sheets of blotter. Before leaving he handed me a brand-new British passport which had been issued a week earlier. Call it a woman's instinct but Eleanor was nervous and tense. From the balcony, she noticed two men in a parked car across the street. By the time I went to check the car was gone.

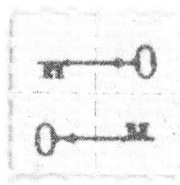

SNARED

I repeatedly knocked on the heavy oak door of the headmaster's office. But there was no reply. Nobody was there! It was no longer 1964

My eyes opened and the police's encirclement remained steadfast. The legislative backbone of the United Kingdom's arcane war on drugs has undergone very few amendments since it was originally drafted into law. I had a rudimentary understanding of the Misuse of Drugs Act 1971 having previously familiarized myself with its contents. With its employment of insipid cryptic legal jargon, it's unlikely to reach a literary best-seller list, but for wannabe dope dealers, it makes for essential reading. Over the past fifty-odd years, the original legislation has undergone several amendments and reclassifications. For example, at one time, simple possession of magic mushrooms was a contravention of the law until it was pointed out that psychoactive fungi grow everywhere, including the grounds of the monarch's estates. This would have made Queen Elizabeth technically in possession of a class-A drug. Consequently, the law was amended to only refer to 'intended cultivation' or 'preparation' of magic mushrooms. Although LSD shares a similar classification status, class A, as its organic cousin, the magic mushroom, sentencing seems to be much harsher. Seeing as how the drug is a non-toxic, non-addictive compound it is baffling to understand why legislators ever felt it necessary to include it in the same category as heroin and cocaine. With hardly any LSD-related deaths ever recorded, I have yet to hear a cogent argument to support the case for its severe classification. Nevertheless, until such time as LSD comes in from the cold and is properly reviewed, those caught intending on supplying the drug could, in the UK, face penalties up to life in prison.

Whilst in the company of the arresting officers, I slowly treaded the faded burgundy carpet up to the front door of the first-floor apartment at number thirteen. I was frantically trying to recall the relevant details of the UK's Misuse of Drugs Act, but everything felt surreal. Prudence would lean towards saying nothing when questioned until first seeking legal advice. The reality was that I had rented an apartment in which I was currently storing a huge consignment of dipped and undipped blotter paper and a hitherto overlooked eye dropper, presumably containing a quantity of a class-A drug. Alternatively, I could say that someone else had left the paper and drugs on the premises and I was unaware of the contents of the boxes stored in the bedroom. I could add that that person was to collect everything later, but the likelihood of convincing a jury of that version of events seemed highly improbable. Besides, allowing that individual to return and collect the items later meant I was technically in possession, and, therefore, I would be supplying them with the drugs and paper.

Before entering the apartment, one of the officers asked if he could expect to find any illegal drugs on the premises. I had yet to be cautioned, so whatever reply I gave would probably be inadmissible in a court of law. I hadn't had time to consider how the situation had arisen. My first concern was to initiate some form of damage limitation control and, at the same time, steer the police firmly in my direction and away from any gruelling interrogation of Eleanor.

"Were there any drugs on the premises?" Who was fooling whom? They knew who I was, where I lived, what was on the premises and, more significantly, who I was involved with. Eleanor's astute observation the night before of the two mysterious men across the street suddenly took on a more ominous perspective. How long had we been under surveillance?

My relaxed demeanour had helped to ease the earlier tension shown by the police. With surgical-gloved hands, the arresting team began trawling every nook and cranny of the apartment. There seemed no point in delaying the inevitable and having the flat ransacked unnecessarily, so I calmly mentioned the location of the stored paper. I claimed responsibility for the design of the image and was commissioned to provide the finished sheets of paper. I overheard an officer transmit a message that the press and media would be arriving shortly. The whole operation had been meticulously planned down to the last detail.

Already the picture was becoming clearer. I had 'confessed' to being a graphic designer responsible for a 'bicycle' image imprinted onto several thousand sheets of absorbent paper, but what was puzzling was there was no serious enquiry regarding any drug, but the police's focus was firmly on the paper. The more I listened to their inquisitiveness the more it became apparent that any drug would play a minor role in the drama. I had even forgotten the remaining forty-odd hits of Ted's private reserve acid that was wedged inside my wallet. Something didn't quite add up. Everything felt low-key and gentil as if we were about to sit down for afternoon tea. Before being led away I politely asked if the formalities of handcuffs could be waived. The head of the arresting team smiled and nodded his approval.

Seated next to a burly detective sergeant in the back seat of an unmarked car, I was being driven to Edmonton, North London, the headquarters of the National Regional Crime Squad. The two officers in the front seats seemed oblivious to my presence, engrossed as they were in the weekend performance of their beloved Arsenal football team. Throughout my life, I have continued to suffer from a serious and embarrassing psychological and social flaw. I can never remember people's names! I can recall in remarkable detail previous conversations, encounters and faces, but for some reason, I am rarely able to recollect names. I glanced at the sergeant and remembered he had accompanied the Englishman that day in August when I handed over the photographs for my replacement passport. It had been thirty years since I last saw a necktie that the sergeant wore that day in the pub. The same knitted woollen tie he was now sporting. It had been my fifteenth birthday, and for a gift, my beloved aunt had sent me a hideous maroon ribbed woollen tie that unaccountably had been the height of fashion at the time. Understandably, plain-clothed detectives try to conceal their profession, but the sergeant's tie was to me, as good as a neon sign. I had been under surveillance for at least six weeks, and another piece of the puzzle had dovetailed into place. When I was informed that we would be making a brief stop in Soho, the last place I expected to pull up was outside my sister's apartment. The upstairs accommodation was laid out over two floors and above a record store owned and operated by a pair of DJs. With no immediate response to the ringing of the doorbell, the sergeant threatened to kick the door down if the store manager failed to provide a spare key. Once inside I was left unguarded whilst the three police officers carried out a routine search. My sister's boyfriend was taking a shower at the time, which explained the unanswered doorbell. He emerged naked from the bathroom to be caught literally and figuratively with his pants down! Lying openly on the coffee table was his personal stash of marijuana which was clearly spotted by the police but ignored.

In the 1956 black and white movie '36 Hours' the actor James Garner plays an American army intelligence officer who is privy to the intended allied invasion of France. Whilst on a routine mission to Portugal, he is drugged and captured by German agents and surreptitiously smuggled out of the country to Nazi Germany. He wakes up in what appears to be a US Army hospital and is told that the war has been over for six years. His doctors inform him that he has been suffering from a rare form of amnesia, and that is the reason he is unable to recall events since the fateful night in Lisbon. His hair and skin appear to have aged, and he is even reunited with his 'wife' whom he was purportedly married to in 1949, the year before. Will the fiendish Nazi imposters be able to extract the details of the invasion from our discombobulated and confused hero in time to thwart the Allies' plans? Whilst shaving in the bathroom Garner notices the miniscule mark on his thumb that he had picked up accidentally cutting himself in the briefing room on the eve of his departure. The simple wound could not have remained unhealed after six years!

The truth sometimes rises to the surface because of the most inconsequential of occurrences. Why, on the occasion that I met the Englishman, had I initially concealed the manila envelope containing the blotter proofs inside my jacket? Why, when I left my sister's apartment, the only time I had visited prior to my arrest, had I elected to carry the envelope in plain sight? Whoever was watching me at the time must have seen me enter and leave and, with the envelope to hand, must have assumed I had collected it from the apartment. There was no other possible reason to search the flat.

The seriousness of the day's events and arrest did not pass without a moment of sublime humour. Following the search the police discovered that their car had been clamped. The psycho sergeant broke into a furious rage venting his anger by kicking the tyre of the car. He set off at pace to admonish the offending parking warden and authorize the clamp's immediate removal. Whilst awaiting his return, I sat uncuffed outside a cafe, sipping a cappuccino in the company of the remaining two officers. Barely two hours had elapsed since what was described by the press as the largest LSD bust in the UK in fifteen years.

By the time we reached Edmonton, the sergeant had managed to regain his composure, and his attitude had transformed dramatically. I was offered a cup of tea but settled for a pen and the Times non-cryptic crossword. I'd never had a reason or inclination ever to visit a police station and now I found myself banged up in one. I stretched out on the concrete bunk and read the stencilled words on the ceiling. 'Crime Stoppers' It was one of those messages inviting the public to grass up a friend or associate. Maybe that had been all the encouragement the Englishman had needed to set me up, but that explanation was too simplistic.

The sergeant returned apologizing profusely that he had only been able to find a copy of the Daily Telegraph. It's not my personal choice of broadsheet and a lousy crossword, but beggars or drug dealers can't be choosers. His transformation from fringe psychopath to a caring human being reeked of insincerity, but he was obviously under orders, but from whom and for what reason? An offer of witness protection was to soon follow. From whom was I to be protected? Apart from the Englishman, I knew no one to fear in the UK. I hadn't lived in the country for nearly two decades. A spectrum of possibilities began to emerge.

It was now apparent that I had been under surveillance for quite some time. The police had shown patience and resolve, waiting until the blotter was ready. They had gone to great lengths, even providing me with a false passport before ensuring the smoking gun, the LSD, was safely in my possession. The Englishman or agent provocateur had at some point been compromised and recruited into the elaborate sting operation. Ted, when he phoned from Prague, had suggested that the LA clients had been arrested, but the Englishman had dismissed the rumour. Was there already a plan in motion when he visited me just before Christmas the previous year? I knew about the US Treasury cash interception, but had others been compromised? Ted's New York client was in jail, and Michael was in custody in Louisiana. Were the American authorities involved in my entrapment here in the UK? There was a scintilla of facts interspersed amongst a mound of speculation that, for the time being, would remain opaque and insoluble.

My first impression of Walter de Groot did not augur well for the prospect of my legal defence. Dressed in an ill-fitting threadbare tweed jacket, wrinkled grey serge trousers and sporting a fake military necktie, he looked like an alcoholic who had just spent a night in the cooler. He reeked of a cocktail of beer and cigarettes, and I had difficulty understanding his heavy Transvaal Afrikaans accent. Behind his thick bi-focal horn-rimmed glasses his eyes looked like giant alien saucers! He muttered in short staccato phrases, and with each word, tiny perspiration droplets would ooze from the pores above his upper lip. I was convinced he was about to suffer a fatal cardiac arrest. Like a vulture about to feed off the scraps from a kill, he nudged the green 'Legal Aid' form across the table and took out a pen from his jacket's inside pocket.

My only immediate access to finances had been the £3500 I had received from the sale of the Range Rover, but the police had already confiscated the money. With no conceivable way of accessing my assets back in California, I would, for the time being, be at the mercy of the UK's legal support system. Allowed one phone call, I had spoken with my sister urging her to seek out legal representation on my behalf. Someone who was experienced in drug-related matters, but for my initial police interview, I would have to rely on Walter's guidance. A duty solicitor was provided by the police.

The two arresting officers, Schilling and the equally balding Welshman, Johnson, conducted the interview whilst Walter remained mute throughout, grinning like a hyena. Counsel might advise prudence and suggest a 'No Comment' response to a preliminary interview but I chose to stick to my role as an artist and designer and see in what direction the questioning might go. The entire proceedings centred around a discussion of blotter, but curiously, there was no mention of the LSD that should have been recovered from the apartment. In fact, there was no mention at all of drugs! They tried to extract information on my blotter production history by constantly referring to my activities in the United States. This was more than curious seeing as I had been arrested on UK soil by British police and facing charges and a possible trial in a UK court.

The two detectives casually mentioned that they had been monitoring my activities for quite some time, so I had to assume they had most of the information they needed. Failing that, I pointed out that all the essential details, names and phone numbers could easily be recovered from my pocket organizer. The officers were taken by surprise and glanced at each other. The recorded interview was brought to an abrupt halt and Johnson hurriedly exited the room. I remember how I had cussed and vented my frustration on recovering the Casio organizer from amongst the damp clothing in the washing machine. I only had myself to blame for not checking my jeans pockets earlier that day. Fortunately, most of the 'lost' information was duplicated in an address book safely stored in San Francisco but for the immediate future I had lost all my contact names and phone numbers. There was an inner sense of amusement at the thought of the fruitless police search for the vital missing evidence. I casually and off the record asked Detective Schilling about the presumed volume of LSD trafficked to the United Kingdom, a figure he estimated to be, on a weekly basis, around 10000 doses. With the LA operation alone being responsible over the previous year for an average of 50,000 doses a week this seemed a remarkable under-estimation on the part of the police. The reality was they had barely scraped the tip of the iceberg.

The following morning, I was led to a parked police sweatbox for transportation to a magistrate's court for a preliminary court appearance. As I climbed aboard, the driver's radio was broadcasting an hourly news update, the details of which included my and Eleanor's arrest and the seizure of ten million pounds of LSD! The court appearance was brief. Within minutes we were both remanded in custody and our bail applications were denied.

Walter de Groot, probably in his eagerness to retain me as a valuable client, had taken the unusual step of inviting a barrister along to the court proceedings, and after a brief reunion with Eleanor in the dock, I was joined by the two defence advocates in a holding cell below the court. The barrister's preliminary assessment of the facts in the case had led him to conclude that I was the apparent victim of a sting operation perpetrated by the British authorities with probable collusion by law enforcement agencies in the United States. Actually, proving an entrapment in a court of law would be an entirely different matter. The police would take all the necessary steps to conceal their modus operandi, including their use of any 'agent provocateur' from both the defence team and the jury. The UK legal system has a very convenient process for providing the police and prosecution with a get-out clause. Invariably, a judge hearing a case involving covert police surveillance operations will grant a 'Public Interest immunity Certificate' allowing for total anonymity. An astute team of lawyers may be able to argue that suppression of evidence would severely jeopardize a defendant from receiving a fair trial, but especially in drug importation and trafficking cases, judges are unlikely to give the defendant the benefit of the doubt. This sobering revelation meant that an alternative and creative strategy would have to be conceived and implemented. In the meantime, I was on my way to Pentonville prison.

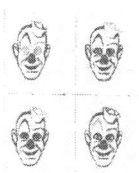

BANGED UP

Understandably there is a natural sense of fear and trepidation that almost anyone would feel, for the first time, on being incarcerated in a prison. How uneasy one might feel locked in a cell with a serial killer or the thought of becoming a sex slave to a 240-pound shaven-headed body-builder. Are all the staff brutal sadists? My first night was an inauspicious encounter with a cellmate who was going through severe heroin withdrawals. Colloquially referred to as 'clucking.' Apart from the moaning and groaning, he took his anguish out on the meagre furniture the cell provided, smashing and breaking a table and two chairs.

In general, the reality of prison life is far removed from Hollywood stereotypes, as one might believe. Most inmates keep to themselves whilst endeavouring to occupy their time in as constructive a way as possible, given the circumstances. Staff try their best, but woefully lacking in funding, the prison service spends most of its time 'plugging the holes with Elastoplast.' The officers come across as disillusioned and seem only eager to escape from jail at the end of their shifts. Unable to find alternative employment the older staff hang on begrudgingly awaiting the inevitable retirement date, a generous pension and their release from self-imposed confinement. My second night on the induction wing was spent bemused by my fellow cellmate's vain attempt to procure a bag of heroin from a cell located two floors above. A plastic drinking cup had been lowered to our barred window by way of a makeshift rope constructed from several strips of bed sheeting tied together. The payment, a prison telephone card, was to be made in advance of the drug's delivery, but with my cellmate failing to come up with his end of the bargain and no immediate credit arrangement on offer, the necessary 'fix' was not forthcoming. The poor guy spent the rest of the night tossing and turning in acute pain. I was just finally dozing off when an officer unlocked the door, and we were ordered out for breakfast. I slipped into my shoes from the top bunk, having been advised not to leave them on the cell floor. Cockroaches have a habit of nesting inside footwear, and the last thing one needs to hear first thing in the morning is a squelch below one's foot. All of the prisoners in the cell block were new inductees on remand and, therefore, permitted to remain dressed in their own clothes. Nevertheless, until this day the overwhelming stench of male body odour remains the enduring bad memory of my time spent in Pentonville.

With all my funds confiscated by the police, I had no way of communicating with the outside world. I approached a prison officer, colloquially referred to as a 'screw,' hoping that his charitable side might provide me with a postage stamp. It seemed like I was a day late as stamps, phone cards, and additional food snacks could only be bought once a week on a Wednesday and today is Thursday. I had a long wait. I was beginning to understand the frustration and sense of hopelessness that inmates endure. The same officer bellowed out an invitation for anyone to join him on the 'R' wing, where education and treatments for drug/alcohol addiction were available. An annual consumption of a few hits of LSD hardly qualified as an addiction, but the offer of education and, therefore, time out of the cell was too good to refuse. Two hours later, I found myself behind the door of a refurbished single cell on the top landing of the 'R' wing. I made a fresh attempt to acquire a postage stamp only to discover that the 'R'wing had already made their weekly visit to the canteen earlier that morning. The earliest I could now expect to get my hands on a precious stamp was a week away!

I was beginning to think that things were going from bad to worse when I was summoned to the wing governor's office and introduced to the towering figure of Senior Officer Ryan. The S.O., having spent twenty years in the prison service, had done his time and was due to retire in less than twelve months. Having offered me a luxurious cup of instant coffee, Ryan proceeded to outline his intentions to open and run the first fully-fledged prison service rehabilitation programme. To date, funds were limited, but if the Home Office could be shown that such a programme was running successfully, then more money would be made available.

"You seem a level-headed and intelligent man. Could I interest you in editing a rehab magazine during your stay on the wing? Having looked at your file I would guess that you'll probably be staying with us for quite some time!"

I could tell that Ryan's sarcasm wasn't intended to be malicious, and with the charges I was facing:

"CONSPIRACY TO MANUFACTURE LSD."

"CONSPIRACY TO SUPPLY LSD"

POSSESSION WITH INTENT TO SUPPLY LSD

I was looking at the prospect of fourteen years to life. Unable to sleep the night before, I spent most of the time wading through the prison regulations manual, so I already had a reasonable understanding of how the system functioned.

"I'll need daily access to a computer, an inter-prison visit to Holloway to see my girlfriend. She's a United States citizen who was over here for a visit, and I'm naturally concerned for her wellbeing .... oh, and a first-class stamp if you have one?"

An expression of mild shock and irritation spread across Ryan's face.

IPVs, or Inter-Prison Visits, are only sanctioned once an inmate has been sentenced to a minimum of six months. I already knew this, but there was no harm in trying.

At two o'clock the following afternoon I was in the back of a mini-cab, handcuffed and sandwiched between two 'screws' on the one-mile journey along the Caledonian Road to the women's prison Holloway. Eleanor couldn't believe her eyes as we were reunited in the visit centre of the women's jail. It had been less than four days since our arrest, and somehow, I had managed, at great expense to the British taxpayer, to get a mini-cab and two members of Her Majesty's Pentonville Prison Staff to take me to visit my girlfriend. Beyond the genuine concern I felt for Eleanor's predicament, the meeting gave us the opportunity to dovetail our stories. So far, she had made a 'No Comment' statement in her police interview and had been advised by her legal counsel to deny any knowledge of the incriminating evidence discovered at the Kensington apartment. I explained that I had revealed to the police my involvement in the design of the paper and how I had deduced that the Englishman had been actively involved in the entrapment that had resulted in our arrest. We parted, reassured, happy and privileged to have had an opportunity to see and speak to one another, longing for the moment when we would be reunited. Alas! In the dock of the Magistrate's Court the following Wednesday. The court appearance was the customary formality and we left, remanded in custody for a further month.

By now, I had begun work in earnest on the rehab magazine and had interviewed several of Pentonville's recovering addicts. Their many harrowing tales had been proofread and edited and were to form the basis of the magazine's first edition. With the magazine work ahead of schedule, I took the opportunity to use the prison computer facilities to work on a few blotter designs. When quizzed by staff members, I merely explained that I was working on a design for a poster for the education department. Nobody was any the wiser and even I had great difficulty in understanding how I was sitting in prison involved in the very activity that got me there in the first place.

A legal visit from De Groot in mid-October broke the tedium that had already set in, but the news he brought was the first break I had been waiting for. The arresting officers had made a tentative approach to my counsel with a request for a further interview and debrief. There was an indication that American officials would wish to attend and were prepared to fly to the UK if I agreed to a meeting. The first clear indication of collusion between British and American authorities was beginning to surface but somehow, I still needed to extract further proof of their collaboration. What remained baffling was who or what they possibly believed I knew. Of the few tenuous connections I had, most of the players, except for Ted, were already in custody or imprisoned.

A carefully orchestrated meeting with the police was set up within the prison, the outcome of which was that I would be surreptitiously smuggled out of prison and taken to a covert location for interrogation. I would be absent from Pentonville for forty-eight hours, which would create a massive internal issue on my return. How would I explain my absence? My only condition was that the police would not oppose a bail application on behalf of Eleanor at our next magistrate's appearance. Unbeknown to me at that time was the fact that officers from the Regional Crime Squad had been searching my assets in San Francisco and had already visited Eleanor's parents in Southern California to persuade their daughter to turn on me. In November, Eleanor was granted conditional bail after her parents posted a surety of $10,000, and the following week, under conditions of heightened secrecy and security, I was taken from Pentonville to the interrogation unit located in Epping Forest. The building, a flat-roofed bungalow surrounded by a ten-foot-high concrete wall capped with an electrified fence, was hidden from prying eyes by a dense copse of woodland. Strategically located and concealed was an array of closed-circuit television cameras that monitored any movement in and outside the facility. Uniformed police officers stationed both inside and outside the compound guarded the unit around the clock.

The American visitors had been delayed by a day, so on the first morning, I was given a thick leather-bound voluminous folder and asked where possible to identify and categorize the contents.

Arranged on each page, not unlike a stamp album, were numerous examples of shards of LSD blotter sheets that had been seized by the police over the previous twenty years. There were pages and pages of blotter pieces. Some of the patterns had found their way into the 'curator's' collection, and there were naturally my own blotter images but the vast majority I was totally unfamiliar with. I needed to demonstrate that I knew much more about the artwork, but the reality was I was groping in the dark and would have to bluff my way through the proceedings. The fact that the police obviously knew very little, if not nothing at all, would work in my favour.

To begin with, I placed the blotters into two categories. Those perforated into quarter-inch squares and those that followed a metric system the majority of which measured ten millimetres. The logic was straightforward. An imperial measurement of a quarter inch could only have originated in the UK, the United States, Canada, Australia, New Zealand or South Africa. The remaining metric pieces could have been produced anywhere else in the world. I could break the groupings down further based on the image. For example, the Japanese Crest could have originated in Japan. (It was from the West Coast of America). Others I randomly connected geographically. Once I had correlated all the information, I set about constructing a family tree with imaginary names, labels and dates and, using coloured pencils and inks, reconstructed an encyclopaedia of blotter.

The Americans arrived the following morning and everyone seemed more than impressed with my creation. The questioning centred completely on my personal involvement as an artist and designer of blotter but my inability to provide any information regarding other individuals, especially since the disappearance of my Casio organizer, left my inquisitors disheartened. Nevertheless, my beautifully constructed almanac of the history of LSD blotter was something that would impress the American's superiors.

As my legal counsel, De Groot was permitted to be present at the interrogation, but any enthusiasm he initially showed soon waned when, after an hour into the second-morning session, he fell asleep and began snoring. The British police were more interested in the importation of LSD into the United Kingdom, but much to their consternation, I put their agent provocateur, the Englishman, firmly in the frame as the UK's LSD kingpin. They were beginning to realize that to entrap me, they had granted immunity to the UK's major importer of LSD. This raised the question of why it was necessary to ensnare me in the first place. The answer, of course, was that I was at that time the sole producer of blotter paper, something that I could legally be arrested for in England but not the United States. There was the minor matter of the Floridian from Panama City for whom I had arranged 2000 hits and who, on his arrest, had dropped my name in the frame, but I wasn't about to be extradited back to the States over such a small issue.

Within two days I was back inside Pentonville where I was quizzed by a couple of inmates over my absence, which I claimed was down to additional charges. One individual, who was facing a murder charge, seemed unconvinced and began spreading a rumour that I would be 'going Q.E.' (Queen's Evidence) and would be giving evidence against my co-defendant. Fortunately, the wing 'Don's' wife was locked up in Holloway with Eleanor and knew that she was merely an innocent victim of my crimes. The situation returned to normalcy and the rumour-monger was moved off the 'R' wing.

That first Friday in December had been routine, like any other day in prison. I'd spent most of the time in the computer room working on the third edition of the rehab magazine. I returned to my cell late afternoon, just in time for the last meal of the day. Over the last month, I had turned vegetarian primarily to avoid the gristle-based stews concocted from some unidentifiable animal. The veggie burger, thrown together with carrot, swede and turnip, wasn't a great improvement, and that evening my appetite had deserted me. I had just flushed the contents of my dinner plate down the toilet when a screw unlocked my cell door. I was ordered to collect my belongings and to accompany him to the prison gate, where I was to be released from custody. I had miraculously been granted bail.

I had already used up my bail application allocations, so how was I suddenly and unexpectedly granted bail?

Greeting me at the prison gate was the inane grinning solicitor De Groot who informed me that my remand custody time limit had expired and mistakenly the Crown prosecution had failed to file for an extension. Severe bail restrictions had been imposed but they paled in comparison to time behind bars. That unexpected newfound freedom was to be short-lived.

THE PLOT THICKENS

I had chosen not to divulge to Eleanor the events that had unfolded behind the scenes, especially my covert meetings with the American authorities. Isolated as she was from friends and family back home in California, she was beginning to feel the strain of her ordeal. When the news arrived that her fingerprints had been found on the glass Pasteur pipette and dropper provided by the Englishman, her spirits hit an all-time low. I assured her that if a plea bargain was in the offering, I would offer up a guilty plea in exchange for her release.

December 25th was less than two weeks away and neither of us was in a festive mood. To raise our spirits, we took a walk along London's Regent Street, taking in the traditional seasonal streetlights. We stopped in a local pub, but Eleanor's anxieties only increased when she spotted a patron who she was convinced had been tailing us earlier that afternoon. We scurried from the scene and headed in a northerly direction. As we stood on the curb waiting for the traffic signal to change to green, I really thought my eyes were deceiving me. I continued to stare at the familiar figure across the street. I just couldn't believe that I was about to come face to face with Steve, my Florida connection. Outwardly, he seemed genuinely relieved to see that we were both no longer in prison, but he didn't seem surprised that we should have bumped into one another. I felt a nagging sense of unease but couldn't quite put my finger on the root cause of my discomfort. As far as I knew, Steve had been busted on a minor cocaine possession charge in Miami and deported from the country. What I was to hear contradicted that information. According to Steve, he had entered a drug rehabilitation programme in California and had taken up residence with my ex-partner, Lindy. Why would anyone on a drug charge in Florida enter a rehab programme in California? Steve's questioning and probing became more specific centred around contacts of mine that I was unaware he had any prior knowledge of. I played dumb, dismissing any connections with the names introduced into the conversation. Steve became ill at ease, twitchy and nervous. He kept glancing furtively over my shoulder, but it appeared he had seen a familiar face. As he left momentarily to visit the toilet, I took the opportunity to scan the room. My encyclopaedic facial recognition attribute recognized at once the young man seated in the far corner of the bar. It was the driver from the unmarked police car that had taken me to Edmonton on the day of my arrest! I instructed Eleanor to hurry from the pub and arrange to meet up at the bail hostel later.

A statistician could probably come up with a set of great mathematical odds of my accidentally bumping into Steve in Central London, especially so soon after my surprise release from prison. Toss into the equation the improbability of the Florida authorities sending a known illegal alien to rehabilitate in California, where he was to reside in my apartment, and I seriously thought I had a better chance of winning the lottery. I will never know for certain, but I remain firmly convinced that Steve was wired, and our 'chance' encounter had been orchestrated.

Our case was due for a committal hearing at Magistrates Court on December 20th, the outcome of which would determine whether we were to stand trial in Crown Court. The very nature of the charges we faced guaranteed that, down the road, we would have to face a jury trial in the upper court of law. However, the magistrate's appearance gave us the first opportunity to pose questions to the witnesses for the prosecution. Only the evidence of two would be required. Firstly, the psycho sergeant who had supervised the search of my sister's apartment and last but not least, the forensic scientist who had compiled the report on the LSD found in the Kensington apartment. I had poured over the twenty-page report and statement whilst on remand in Pentonville and had discovered an anomaly or contradiction that could be exploited. I had briefed my barrister on the line of questioning to take, none of which made sense to him but I assured counsel that if my hunch was right, we might be able to expose a flaw in the forensic examination. During the Epping Forest interrogation, the police were curious to know the significance of a pocket ultraviolet strip lamp that had been recovered from my hold-all. LSD glows an iridescent blue, not unlike traces of blood when exposed to ultraviolet. Over-exposure was inadvisable as it would cause the compound to degrade rapidly and thereby render it inactive. Common forensic practice will use gas chromatography and mass spectrometry to separate the different compounds present in a chemical sample and, therefore, identify precisely each element. An amount of heat is involved in the process of using an inert gas. A commonly known fact concerning LSD is that when exposed to light, heat or moisture the compound will degrade. All we needed to do was to show to a layman, Justice of the Peace, that the exposure of the prosecution's physical evidence to heat would contaminate the samples. Of course, in reality, the heat involved would have a negligible effect, but the sitting justice wouldn't know that. The expert witness stated that it was remote but nevertheless possible for heat to transform the compound into another chemical. The scientist was beginning to understand how the line of questioning had spread doubt and contradiction into his statement. The Crown Prosecution Service barrister had the opportunity to cross-examine, but the very nature of the questioning left her out of her depth, and the witness stood down. The psycho sergeant's replies to his questioning were even more embarrassing than the expert scientific witness. He denied any knowledge of the British passport in the name of Christopher Brian Morrison recovered from the Kensington flat and refused to answer the question when asked if he had previously been aware of the passport's existence. He then denied having seen either Eleanor or me prior to our arrest.

The committal hearing was abruptly ended, and moments later the case was passed to Wood Green Crown Court for further hearings and procedures. As there was now technically a legal change in my circumstances with the case committed to Crown Court, it would be necessary to reapply for bail. I was assured that as I was already out on bail, the application would be a mere formality. The prosecution opposed bail and without my counsel being permitted to argue the case, bail was denied. I was on my way back to Pentonville and my first prison Christmas. The tactics we had employed in the hearing had flustered the police, who had expected me to be compliant. I was cornered in a holding cell by the arresting officers where I denied any foreknowledge of my counsel's tactics, but I expressed my intention to have them replaced.

De Groot was shocked to receive his marching orders especially as he was about to relinquish a huge fee for such a high-profile case. I was waiting to be shown back to my cell when into the room walked a dishevelled, bearded, petite lawyer sporting a Jimi Hendrix hairstyle and a floral shirt. There was encrusted dirt beneath his fingernails and on his feet, he wore a pair of shoddy open-toed sandals. Soap and water seemed an anathema to him. Anyone passing the briefing room could be forgiven for assuming that I was the lawyer and he was the inmate.

I gave a brief account of my circumstances and without commenting Michael Katz pulled from a faded tan satchel a hardback copy of a book entitled:

"HUNTING MARCO POLO"

I returned to my cell, and for the next day, I buried myself in the story of the dramatic attempts by law enforcement agencies worldwide to bring to justice an international drug smuggler by the name of Howard Marks. The book was both absorbing and entertaining, but I couldn't understand why Katz had passed it to me. There were some parallels with my background but there was no real comparison with my current legal situation.

Michael Katz duly arrived for the pre-arranged legal visit the following week, attired in the same 'uniform' he outlined to me his former role as Mark's defence attorney and his efforts to thwart the DEA's attempt to extradite the drug smuggler from Spain to stand trial in Florida on cannabis importation charges. Michael's story was a long and protracted account and probably due to his ADHD, he kept losing the thread mid-sentence and would constantly have to begin again. Again, it seemed that our roles were reversed with *I* as the legal counsel listening to his statement. It was not exactly encouraging but he held bona fide legal qualifications as both an American attorney and a UK solicitor. Essential qualities in unravelling the complexities of my case. He was well aware of the difficulties in communicating with the outside world from the confines of prison, so he arranged for me a prepaid telephone account on the outside. A service that was to prove invaluable over the next few months. In Britain's prisons between 1987 and 2004, British Telecom made available BT Phonecards, which could be used by prisoners in cardphone payphones. Twenty- or forty-unit cards could be purchased for £2.00 and £4.00 respectively. Inexplicably the credits would always expire far quicker than when using an equivalent card outside. Any attempt should the need arise, to telephone long distance would prove futile as the credits would be gobbled up post-haste. In addition, most direct calls would be monitored by the staff. Using my account, I could bypass the prison security by simply calling the account's London number and entering a predetermined PIN code; I could then dial anywhere in the world for the cost of just one unit on my phone.

Random searches of the contents of inmates' cells, colloquially referred to as 'spins,' are routines carried out extensively and thoroughly by internal security with closer scrutiny paid to prisoners either facing or convicted of drug offences. On the 'R' wing, these degrading experiences took place with increasing regularity to flush out inmates abusing or relapsing whilst undergoing their rehabilitation. A compulsory drug-testing programme was yet to be introduced and cell spins were believed to be the only effective method for stemming the ever-increasing use of drugs in jail. In previous searches, no effort was made to remove the computer floppy discs I had in my possession, but suddenly, they constituted a threat to security. The information recorded was a draft for the next edition of the rehab magazine and an original blotter design that I had just completed.

The continuing tedium of life behind bars was briefly interrupted by an unexpected court appearance. De Groot had filed a motion contesting my right to change my legal representation. He was trying to persuade a judge to overrule the matter of his dismissal and have him reinstated as my counsel. The judge denied the appeal. In early March, a trial date was set for mid-June, and the prosecution successfully applied, ex parte, for Public Interest Immunity to be granted regarding the undisclosed evidence. All the covert information regarding surveillance, the use of an agent provocateur, any involvement of overseas law enforcement agencies and the entrapment details would be barred from the defence counsel and an appointed jury.

Through a California intermediary, I was to learn that a British undercover officer, whose description resembled the balding Welshman, Johnson, had visited the curator in San Francisco. Posing as my friend, he was attempting to acquire a batch of LSD using blotter paper ostensibly designed by me. Unbeknown to the officer and his DEA cohorts, the 'Curator' had been ostracized by the LSD community. He had continued to hold a red rag to a bull by goading the authorities over his self-promotion of LSD blotter art. The collapse, the previous year, of the authorities' attempt to have him put on trial in Texas must have severely dented the ego of Artie Hubbard, the DEA's LSD task force's tzar; the attempted set-up proved fruitless for three reasons. Firstly, the curator never had access to supplies of LSD. Secondly it was glaringly obvious that Johnson, dressed the way he was, was unlikely to be a friend of mine and thirdly, the blotter design featuring the logo for the 1994 Football World Cup was a farcical concept to begin with.

Using the established phone link, I had already contacted a friend in San Francisco who had removed any incriminating evidence from my apartment, including the address book containing my contact lists.

On her final visit to Pentonville Eleanor was reluctant to accept my belief that we had a good chance of busting the case. Unable to share my optimism, she left in a despondent mood, dreading the ordeal of the court and trial that was scheduled for the following week. Katz had recruited the services of leading counsel in the person of Tafiq Kouri Q.C. who would argue on my behalf for the evidence withheld under the P.I.I. (Public Interest Immunity) A certificate is to be made available to the defence. If his arguments failed to persuade the judge, then we had a backup plan waiting to be used if called upon.

There are an infinite number of more pleasurable life experiences than appearing in the dock of a Crown Court, but that June morning, I was genuinely looking forward to the theatre of the occasion and the drama that was about to unfold. My confidence proved infectious, and for the first time, Eleanor appeared calm and relaxed. Our respective barristers had met the conference earlier so her team was aware of any move or tactic my counsel was prepared to employ, if necessary.

Kouri was a striking figure neatly attired in an immaculately tailored dark pinstriped suit and customized Jermyn Street shirt beneath his formal robes. His dark, bushy moustache was perfectly groomed, and with flashes of grey in his hair, he bore a remarkable resemblance to the Egyptian actor Omar Sharif. If style counted for anything then he stood head and shoulders above the prosecution barrister. There was only one point of law to discuss and that revolved around disclosure of unused material to be made available to the defence. Kouri articulated his objections immaculately but what was even more remarkable was that he spent a whole day delivering his argument. His performance was more like a filibuster as he managed to labour over the same issue hour after hour but never quite repeating himself. He even eloquently presented a pocket history of LSD to the court erring on only one occasion when he referred to the discoverer of the drug as Alfred Hofmann instead of Albert, an unfortunate mistake that was amazingly rectified by the judge, who had obviously done his homework. As Kouri repeatedly enunciated the relevant points of law, the judge sat sagely nodding, but it was becoming increasingly more and more apparent that despite the Queen's Counselor's valiant effort, the withheld evidence would not be made available. Just before lunch on the second day, Kouri finally sat down, and the judge ruled in favour of the prosecution. None of the information relating to my entrapment would be permitted during the trial, and the time had arrived to swear in the jury.

Kouri leapt to his feet and requested an immediate adjournment. The judge was taken by surprise. Why was it suddenly necessary after a lengthy nine-month wait, during which the defence had had adequate time to prepare its case?

"My lord, perhaps in anticipation that your decision would not prove favourable to my client, and, seeing as how this case undoubtedly involves the United States Federal Bureau of Investigation and the United States Drug Enforcement Agency, counsel for the defence has already filed in a Federal Court in Washington D.C. a motion for the withheld evidence to be released under America's Freedom of Information Act. Therefore we feel unable to proceed until the requested information is released by the United States Government!"

The bombshell delivered had caught the court off-guard, so an immediate recess was called, and both prosecution and defence counsels were summoned to the bench. Eleanor and I returned to the basement holding cells to await the outcome of the deliberations. I had expected a lengthy discussion between the advocates, so I was surprised when a smiling Kouri arrived at my cell door barely ten minutes later.

The prosecution had offered a deal. I was to switch my plea to guilty. All charges against Eleanor would be dropped and it was agreed that the judge would set a maximum tariff of four years. A four-year sentence meant I would have to serve a minimum of thirty-two months before applying for parole. Having already served nine months on remand I would remain incarcerated for a further twenty-three months. Alternatively, If I were to await the outcome of the undisclosed evidence through the US courts, I would probably be sitting on remand for a further two years, and Eleanor would also have to remain in England on bail during that period, an ordeal that seemed hardly fair on her.

My response was swift and to the point:

"You can go back and tell them that if the sentence is less than four years and they return all the confiscated cash, then they have a deal. Oh! At the same time, you can ask them whether or not the United States Immigration and Naturalization Service is aware that a British police officer travelling on a false passport recently entered the country in a DEA-instigated plan to compromise a United States citizen."

Kouri was shocked that I was attempting to blackmail the court, but I assured him that it was a simple case of entrapment! Kouri was back downstairs in five minutes with the offer of a three-and-a-half-year sentence. Three and a half with automatic release at the halfway point converted to a maximum of twenty-one months in prison. I entered a guilty plea to a conspiracy charge and with all charges dismissed against Eleanor and the money returned she was able to return safely to California. I had exactly one day under a year to serve

DENOUEMENT

So what became of the kilo of ET, ergotamine tartrate, that I neglected to mention earlier and that I had brought into the UK? Or why was the conical glass flask, left in the Kensington apartment fridge and containing 20 grams of LSD crystal, never retrieved by the police? Or was it? It certainly wasn't presented as evidence! What about the set of laboratory scales left on the mantelpiece? The owner of the apartment had returned from Indonesia shortly after the arrests. Through an intermediary, I received the news that the set of scales was still above the fireplace, but there was no sign of any of the other items. The answers to the remaking questions I will probably never know.

A journey to Prague was to be my first overseas trip after my release from Pentonville. Through Lennar in Amsterdam, I had located Ted in the Czech Republic where he had continued to reside since his flight from California in early 1993 Mingling with a crowd of Italian teenagers on their Easter break, we strolled across the Charles Bridge into the old town and meandered up the hill towards the Royal Palace and St Vitus' Cathedral. I was to learn that a few months before my arrest in London, our former associate, The Babe, had been arrested whilst attempting to sell a quantity of LSD crystal to an undercover narcotics officer posing as a 'Deadhead.' Lightning, in his case, had truly stuck twice! Unable to face further jail time and probably a life sentence, he had put a number of peoples' names in the frame probably including Ted's and mine. What became of him remains a mystery.

Ted had hardly changed in the twenty years since we first met at the Krasnapolsky Hotel in Amsterdam. He still bore the same matted beard, tangled hair and was dressed in the same shabby military fatigues. His modest one-bedroom apartment, located five minutes from Wenceslas Square, looked and smiled like a pig sty and he blew all his money on whoring in the brothels of Prague. It didn't surprise me to learn that wherever we went in town, Ted was on a first-named basis with the ladies of the night. He still managed to put his professional skills to good use, and that afternoon, we took a liberal dose of blotter acid that he had recently synthesized. Regrettably, the acid had been dipped on plain white paper. After an eventful weekend, we parted company at the airport, and I flew back to London. We had both promised to stay in touch, but my letters and phone calls remained unanswered. We never spoke again.

Eleanor took a job with a major German skincare and fragrance company, rising to a position on the board of directors of the US affiliate in less than three years. She remained faithful to me during my last year of incarceration, and we spoke each Sunday morning. On the day of my release she informed me that we would part company and go our separate ways.

In April 2001, the 'Curator' went on trial in Kansas City on a fresh charge of conspiracy to supply LSD. The crux of the US Federal Government's case was that impregnated blotter paper recovered by law enforcement agents had undoubtedly originated in San Francisco and, before impregnation, had formed a part of the curator's extensive collection. The District Attorney's main exhibit consisted of the curator's entire collection of blotter containing some 33.000 sheets of paper of which two hundred had been framed artwork. Under careful forensic examination, none of the sheets of paper were found to contain any trace of LSD, although some of the sheets were identical in design to those originally seized by the authorities. The defence pointed out that blotter art was internationally recognized as a modern form of folk art and that the curator's collection had formed the basis for several exhibitions staged in galleries throughout the world. Under the defence counsel's cross-examination, a renowned critic from New York City argued in favour of the artistic value of blotter paper printed with the FBI logo and numerous other controversial images. The art form employed by various anonymous artists had been responsible over a twenty-year period for the diverse and fascinating collection of work presented before the court. After a twoweek-long trial, the jury agreed with the defence, and the curator was on his way home to San Francisco.

VANITY BLOTTER

The new Millennium has seen an explosion in interest in blotter but it is far beyond the practical use of the previous decades. No longer are the absorbent sheets of paper just intended as a delivery system for illicit LSD, but those decorative sheets have given birth to a whole new art form. Vanity blotter art.

In 2001, I received a phone call from a male with a broad South London accent. Paul 'Monkey' Guest explained that he and a compatriot, Jon Blackburn, who was based in New Orleans, had set up UK and US websites marketing and transacting in sheets of blotter art. He asked me if I wouldn't mind taking a look at the two websites and getting back to him with my impression and opinion.

I was surprised to see the huge variety of blotter images displayed. The majority I had become familiar with over the past decades, but there was now a whole new selection of artwork available to view and purchase. What I found particularly exciting was that the public was now able to witness entire blotter sheets, something that, in the past, virtually nobody apart from the supplier of mass quantities of LSD would have been able to view. Bear in mind that as LSD blotter passes down the supply chain in ever-decreasing amounts, only snippets or shards of the original complete design are all that remain. Now, suddenly, the work that fellow blotter artists and I had produced was available for all and sundry to see, hopefully, admire and, in the case of the two vanguard blotter art dealers, to sell.

There were already some noticeable differences between the original underground blotter and these new designs, which collectively have come to be known as 'Vanity' blotter art. Rather than a repeated icon covering each perforated square, they were now decorated with a single image covering an entire sheet. There were reproductions of familiar artworks by such artists as Andy Warhol, and even Da Vinci's 'Mona Lisa' had fallen foul to perforation into 900 quarter-inch squares!

When approached by 'Monkey' to produce some new blotter designs, I was initially reticent, as for me, blotter simply served one purpose, and as yet, I couldn't envisage it becoming a viable artform. After much soul-searching, I acquiesced and provided the two blotter dealers with a pair of limited editions, each of fifty sheets, both of which I numbered and signed under the nom de plume of 'Barrie Bonds.' I elected not to use my real name, as having served time for the possession of three thousand sheets of blotter paper, putting my signature on further sheets of blotter seemed like showing a red rag to a bull! An additional design was commissioned the following year, but my artwork was heading in a new direction, and I ceased working on any further blotter work.

It had been two years since I last heard from 'Monkey' so I was surprised when, out of the blue, he telephoned just before Christmas 2005. An LSD symposium was to take place between January 13th and 15th, 2006, which would include a celebration of the discoverer of LSD, Albert Hofmann's 100th birthday. The event, at that time, was to be the largest psychedelic event ever held in the world and experts in the field, from all points of the compass, would be participating in numerous lectures and forums.

Once we had disembarked from the cross-channel car ferry, Monkey and I drove through the night arriving outside Basel's Convention Centre early on the morning of January 13th, 2006. For the first time in thirteen years, I was reunited with the 'Curator', who would be giving a 'PowerPoint' presentation of a selection of blotters from his private collection.

I was mingling with the crowd in the reception hall where a man in his mid-thirties was introduced to me. Dieter was a Kollegstufe teacher, the equivalent in the UK being six-form secondary education. He smiled enthusiastically but vigorously shook my hand. He proceeded to explain how 13 years previous, he had ingested some of my 'shield' blotters and the very nature of the design had taken him on a mediaeval mystical voyage of discovery. He was convinced that the imagery had been fundamental to the experience he had undergone. Eager to learn more he pressed me further on the origin of the 'shield' 'design.

I had researched mediaeval French noblemen who purportedly were practicing alchemists and incorporated their family crests into the design. The intended analogy is the transformational processes of both base metal in alchemy with that of LSD and the mind. Strange but also rewarding that this has been the only occasion that someone has reported to me directly the details of the encounter they had undergone after ingesting a piece of my finished artwork!

Over the years, there has been a hotly debated issue over when exactly the official 'bicycle day' Should be celebrated. 'Bicycle Day,' the first controlled LSD experiment, is now annually celebrated throughout the world on April 19th, although the first accidental ingestion of LSD by its discoverer, Albert Hofmann, occurred three days earlier on April 16th. My personal preference has always been the earlier date as my '50th Anniversary' blotter bears the date 'April 16th' and on that day in 1993, I am my travelling partner, dropped 500 mics of 'Special Reserve Shield' blotter and set off on a bicycle ride along the north coast of Crete. The event has developed a cult following, with celebrations occurring in the United States, Europe, South America and Australia.

Blotter art websites have sprouted over the world and even highly respected artists have turned their talents to designing blotter. Various Facebook groups specializing in blotter art command memberships in the tens of thousands. Only recently have I personally turned my attention back to designing blotter which coincidentally has given me a new lease on life. To this day, I have always wondered where those minuscule examples of my artwork ever ended up. All those millions of shields and other designs. In the last six months, the question has been answered by way of social media. From New York to the UK to Goa in India to Australia and New Zealand, positive feedback has returned after 30 years.

Here is a message I received in May 2023 from an individual who was at the conception and emergence of the Psytrance music and cultural movement in Goa around 1990.

"Those shields really impressed me at the time and still do today. They have made me laugh like fuck in some dark times through them connecting us and recalling some of those stories. Most would never believe it but I swear they are all true and need no exaggeration. Toning down for most sensitive folks, maybe. The bunch of 1000s of people who got high for free all at the same time, on my punch and were then obliged to listen to my trippiest night asylum sets under the stars, never got to see how beautiful those shields were but at the end of the party, they had felt their power in the colours, the bass and their minds. I never knew most of them, never met before or after, but we shared an experience, a fucking good experience, one I'll always remember, and I'm sure they all will too."

JOURNEYING IN THE FUTURE

The publication of 'BLOTTO' marks precisely sixty years since my first encounter with LSD. Throughout those last six decades I have continued, in

one way or another, to support the inalienable moral right for humankind to freely investigate and use psychedelics whether organic or synthetic. I chose to stand up against what I believed was an unjust law regarding their use and like many pioneering psychonauts before and after me, sacrificed my liberty.

We are now living in exciting times where the whole subject of psychedelics is starting to come in from the cold. More and more funding is being poured into researching the benefits, both medically and scientifically, of psychedelics, and there is a greater chance that the legalization of LSD, In one form or another, may actually become a reality in my lifetime.

My personal contribution in terms of keeping the flame of LSD burning throughout the years amounts to barely a scintilla but at a recent event, an interesting hypothesis was pointed out to me. I was invited to attend the biennial 'Boom' festival held in an isolated location 150 miles north of Lisbon, Portugal. Primarily a music event, the festival has expanded over the last 26 years into what is referred to as a 'transformational, multidisciplinary, psychedelic and sustainable festival. Music still performs the predominant role of the seven-day experience; however whole areas of the site were given over to wellness activities such as yoga, water therapy, meditation and medicinal sessions. There were also healthy eating workshops and holistic classes in food sustainability. There were naturally markets trading in jewelry and clothing and live painting sessions provided by a diverse collection of 'visionary artists.'

I hadn't attended a festival for several years, so I was initially shy and uncomfortable at the thought of being able to properly communicate with festival-goers two generations behind me. I kept asking myself what a seventy-six-yer-old was doing at an event primarily aimed at a crowd fifty years younger than myself. All my worries and concerns were soon put to rest. I have overlooked one basic fact, which was that the attendees were a like-minded collection of individuals, and their warmness and camaraderie towards one another dissolved all existing social boundaries. People were

constantly smiling and greeting each other as if they were long-lost friends. The atmosphere of positivity and warmth was truly remarkable and infectious. What did these forty thousand festival-goers have in common that had drawn them to this isolated lakeside location in the middle of nowhere, and what is Psytrance music all about?

It would be a reasonable assumption to suggest that psychedelic substances were a common factor and integral part of not just 'Boom' but all of the psytrance festivals that have emerged worldwide over the years.

Psytrance music's roots can be traced back to the rave scene of the Indian state of Goa in the early 1990s. Travellers and hippies have been visiting the region since the late 1960s. Traditional early psychedelic music such as Pink Floyd or Grateful Dead would be played by DJs but by the time House music appeared in the late 1980s, the Goa scene had already begun transforming

Its music into a stylized individual electronic dance music, which became known as Goa trance. From those early days, psytrance's shoots have grown and the music has blossomed into numerous forms and styles. Major festivals based on the theme of psytrance now takes place not only in Goa but Europe, Brazil, South Africa,

Australia and perhaps the most famous event, although technically a psychedelic gathering not a psytrance festival, 'Burning Man' is held annually in the remote Black Rock Desert, a remote area north of Reno, Nevada, USA.

Back in July 2023, very early one morning, whilst sitting alone in 'Boom's' artist encampment, I was joined at the table by a convivial Portuguese character. There was no one else around, with most party-revellers trying to catch up on their sleep. Over a coffee, I struck up a conversation with the man, Nuno, who, to my amazement, turned out to be one of the individuals responsible for the staging of 'Boom.' It was fascinating to hear an encapsulated version of the festival's history, especially from one of the event's pioneers. As eager as I was to learn about Nuno, he was equally keen to know of my background. I outlined my artistic endeavours, focusing specifically on my LSD blotter work. I mentioned the fact that I had only recently discovered that the final destination of hundreds of thousands of my blotter had been Goa and that for a two-year period, my LSD had been liberally distributed at the various Goa trance happenings. Nuno's eyes lit up, and a broad smile was etched across his face.

"So, it's probable that we wouldn't be here today without the contribution of your LSD. Quite possibly, the whole psytrance movement was inspired by those thousands of small paper squares that left San Francisco and found their way to a former Portuguese colony in India.?"

Given the rapidly expanding interest and rebirth of psychedelics and LSD, I

finally feel I can reflect, despite the hardships, on those years spent in pursuit of spreading and keeping the flame of LSD burning. From an artistic standpoint. What other conceptual art form presents the opportunity, despite its small scale, to view an image, which, following its ingestion, takes you on a whole different, transformative and emotive experience?

Art is not confined just to galleries. It is a fundamental part of our daily lives. Design goes into everything we touch and utilize. The food package in the fridge, the homes we inhabit and the vehicles in which we ride and drive. The psychology of colour is partly what determines which brand we are drawn towards on the supermarket shelf. We decorate our homes according to our personal tastes. We even select the colour of our car. We don't necessarily have a conscious emotional response to these actions. Staring at a Great Master artwork, watching a movie or listening to a piece of music are media that best evoke emotional sentiment. There are various definitions of this perceptiveness, ranging from joy and happiness to fear and anger.

That minute square of artwork laced with LSD can unlock the entire spectrum of emotion during the journey. Many 'travellers' will tell you the encounter has unbounded benefits, and as a blotter artist, I am proud that my art has had such a positive outcome for so many.

ALCHEMY

A.K.A.

SHIELDS

A.K.A.

KNIGHTS OF MALTA

1992

Redeem Your Blotter

To redeem your free blotter please submit by email the following code:

50ANV/1993/5454

(This offer does not include shipping)

Please be sure to include your full name and postal address.

Contact:

kevinbarron@btinternet.com

or

kbarron.co.uk

Made in the USA
Columbia, SC
10 February 2025

86c89fb7-72cc-4009-a704-8b6a4c750939R01